Circuit Hikes in Northern New Jersey

Fifth Edition
2003

by
Bruce Scofield

Maps and photos by the author

NEW YORK-NEW JERSEY TRAIL CONFERENCE 1920

Published by New York-New Jersey Trail Conference
156 Ramapo Valley Road
Mahwah, New Jersey 07430
www.nynjtc.org

Library of Congress Cataloging-in-Publication Data

Scofield, Bruce.
    Circuit hikes in northern New Jersey/by Bruce Scofield.--
5th ed. p. cm.
    ISBN 1-880775-27-1 (pbk.)
    1. Hiking--New Jersey--Guidebooks.   2. New Jersey --
Guidebooks. I. Title.

GV199.42.N5 S26 2001
917.49--dc21

Edited by *Daniel D. Chazin*
Book design, layout and typesetting by *Adrienne Coppola*
Cover design by *Steve Butfilowski*
Cover photo: Wawayanda Furnace, Wawayanda State Park
Key map by *Lou Leonardis*

Although the editor and publisher have attempted to
make the information as accurate as possible, they accept
no responsibility for any loss, injury or inconvenience sus-
tained by any person using this book.

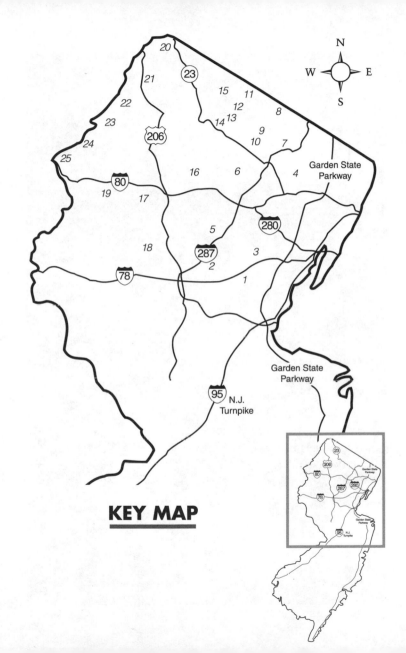

KEY MAP

Table of Contents

Introduction

This guidebook is written for those who wish to explore on foot the many scenic forests, mountains and lakes in northern New Jersey, and who, for the sake of convenience, choose to hike the trails in a circular fashion. Many hikers prefer to walk alone or with just one or two companions, making it difficult to arrange a shuttle from one end of a trail to another. This might not be much of a problem where public transportation is readily available, but it usually isn't in the remote regions containing the most interesting scenery. Besides, using one car reduces the amount of carbon pushed into the atmosphere.

This guidebook also attempts to provide the reader with a wide range of hiking conditions to choose from and offers some detailed particulars about each hike. There are hikes here for children as well as for serious hikers. Variations on each hike — permitting one to lengthen or shorten its distance — are included when appropriate. Additionally, a geological theme should help to familiarize the reader with the differences in terrain on the various hikes.

I have limited myself to describing hikes in northern New Jersey for the following reasons. Interesting walking opportunities exist in the Pine Barrens and along the beaches in South Jersey, but there are few marked trails, and those that do exist are mostly end-to-end trails or short nature trails, neither of which fit into the scheme of this book.

The hikes in this guidebook are the "classic" hikes in northern New Jersey. Why? The first reason is that the reader is guided to every major hiking area in the region. The second is that the hikes described in this book are creatively routed so as to include the most variety and the features of most interest to hikers. This is proven by the fact that many of these routes have been copied — some exactly — in subsequent guidebooks. *Circuit Hikes in Northern New Jersey* was first published in 1984, and it was the first hiking guide to focus exclusively on the northern part of the state.

The sequence of hikes in this guide is based on the geology of North Jersey. Since northern New Jersey is divided by geologists into three distinct provinces, I have used that classification in organizing the hikes. Moving from east to west, we begin with four hikes in the Piedmont Lowlands. Here civilization has made a very deep imprint, and there are few places where one can find the solitude of the forest. Just to the west of the Piedmont Lowlands lies the Highlands Province, which provides miles and miles of excellent hiking opportunities. Here the hiker can find considerable variety in just a few miles. Lakes, swamps, forests and mountains are in abundance, and the area features a surprisingly dense network of trails.

West of the Highlands is the Ridge and Valley Province, which contains the highest elevations in the state. Along the ridge of Kittatinny Mountain runs the Appalachian Trail (A.T.), which extends from Maine to Georgia. Because of the A.T., this area is probably better known as a hiking area than any other in the state. This is unfortunate, because parts of Kittatinny Mountain — such as the Delaware Water Gap and Sunfish Pond area — are overused, while miles of equally interesting and challenging trail go virtually unused just a few miles to the east in the Highlands Province. The elevations in the mountain ridges of the Highlands compare favorably, being only about only two hundred feet lower than the average height of Kittatinny Mountain.

Using this book

Each hike in this book is rated according to its difficulty. The standard is relative: some may find hikes I have rated as "moderate" to be strenuous, while others may not. Hikes with the word "strenuous" in the rating should be considered challenging, not only in a physical sense, but also in terms of pathfinding. These are the hikes that will probably be of the greatest interest to serious hikers. Good "woods sense" and map-reading skills are necessary for these hikes, since portions of the hike may not follow marked trails. The hiking time given is a rough (and relative) estimate of the average time spent on the trail walking, with a few short rest stops — but be sure to give yourself plenty of extra time to observe nature and enjoy the scenery.

The maps in this book are based on United States Geological Survey (USGS) topographic maps. While they show elevations and contours clearly, they do not show all the trails in any given area. Some of them have not been revised for many years and do not show all current changes in the landscape. Moreover, some of them show features that no longer exist and names that are no longer used. These may be of interest to historically minded hikers. Photo-revisions, based on aerial photographs, are included on many of the maps to show new features, such as roads and housing developments.

The overlay on the map clearly shows the route of the hike and major junctions with other trails. This information should get you through the hike easily enough. However, if you are serious about knowing the surrounding terrain and would like to do some exploring, by all means obtain the

Trail Conference maps that are listed in the headings of many of the hikes. These excellent maps are colorful (with public land marked in green) and informative, and they are printed on Tyvek material that is both waterproof and tearproof. Currently available are the two-rnap North Jersey Trails set, which covers trails in the northern parts of Bergen and Passaic counties, and a four-map set for the Kittatinnies. These maps are available at most outdoor stores or directly from the Trail Conference (see contact information below). True map fanatics may also want the USGS topographic maps, which do not show many hiking trails but are invaluable for elevation checking and stream locations. USGS topographic maps can be obtained from some outdoor stores or by mail (for further information, consult the USGS web site, http://mapping.usgs.gov/topomaps). For some of the hikes, maps prepared by the State of New Jersey, Department of Environmental Protection (DEP) or by county park commissions, which show trails and park roads, are available from park headquarters in state and county parks and forests.

For additional information on hiking in New Jersey, consult the *New Jersey Walk Book*, published by and available from the New York-New Jersey Trail Conference. The material in this volume derives from the classic *New York Walk Book*, which has been through seven editions since 1923. In the mid 1990s, it was decided to publish a separate volume for trails in New Jersey. Also recommended is *Fifty Hikes in New Jersey*, written by Stella Green, Neil Zimmerman and myself. This book was first published in 1988, and a new edition was released in 1997. Information about these books and others may be obtained by contacting the New York-New Jersey Trail Conference, 156 Ramapo Valley Road, Mahwah, NJ 07430; (201)512-9348; www.nynjtc.org.

Hiking in Northern New Jersey

Contrary to what many would expect, northern New Jersey offers some of the most varied and interesting day-hiking in the eastern United States. Within this relatively compact region, hikers are able to explore exposed mountain ridges, deep, dark hemlock ravines, and huge swamps. Historical remains — such as old mine shafts, iron-smelting furnaces, Revolutionary War encampments, cellar holes and other evidence of former occupation — make hiking in the area both interesting and educational. There are many opportunities for short as well as longer, more physically demanding hikes. While other regions may have higher summits and more acreage open to the public, few have such variety in such a small area.

Most of the trails described in *Circuit Hikes in Northern New Jersey* are on public land that comprises the many state and county parks and forests. In some areas, a system of trails has been developed, and often the agency in charge publishes a map. A few longer trails exist, however, and these may be of interest to hikers seeking to explore a wider area than that covered by the hikes in this book. These are listed below.

The Appalachian Trail (A.T.) crosses the Delaware River from Pennsylvania and enters New Jersey at the Delaware Water Gap. It then follows the long Kittatinny Ridge in a northeasterly direction for over 40 miles, reaching High Point, the highest elevation in New Jersey. From there it turns east and descends, crossing farmland, wetlands (on bog bridges and boardwalks) and Pochuck Mountain to reach the Highlands. After traversing Wawayanda State Park, it meets Bearfort

Mountain, turns north and heads into New York State. The total length of the Appalachian Trail in New Jersey is about 72 miles.

A number of excellent hikes, some of them described in this book, are possible by utilizing a section of the Appalachian Trail. Primitive camping is permitted in designated areas along the trail, making a backpacking trip possible. Contact park officials for information on current regulations. For more information on the A.T. in New Jersey, consult the *Appalachian Trail Guide to New York and New Jersey*, available from the New York-New Jersey Trail Conference.

The Highlands Trail is a trail-in-the-making. The call for preservation of the New York and New Jersey Highlands has sparked the creation of a long greenway from Storm King Mountain on the Hudson River to Phillipsburg on the Delaware. As of 2003, the northern sections of the trail in New Jersey, from Sterling Forest at the New York state boundary south to Mahlon Dickerson Reservation in Morris County, have been completed. Only a few portions of the remainder of the proposed route in the state are presently open to the public. When completed, the Highlands Trail will be a continuous footpath of about 150 miles. A guide to the Highlands Trail is available from the Trail Conference.

A few other longer trails presently exist in New Jersey. Most of these are multi-use trails, which means that the hiker will have to share the trail with other users, including mountain bikes and horses. The Paulinskill Valley Rail-Trail and Sussex Branch Trail follow abandoned railroad lines that traverse sections of Sussex and Morris Counties. In Morris County, the 20-mile Patriots' Path follows the route of the Whippany River, and also includes several side trails. Portions of this trail are paved for bicycles. One six-mile section of the Patriots' Path — the section that traverses Jockey Hollow — is a true footpath and is of particular interest to hikers. The 20-mile Lenape Trail is another multi-use trail that connects parkland in Essex County. There are plans to link this trail with the Patriots' Path.

Hiking the Trails

In the past, trails were crude foot, horse and wagon routes between two points. An end-to-end concept was established for logical reasons, and this has been retained in many of our modern park and forest trail systems. Many of today's trails are the remnants of old roads that have become overgrown and now are suitable only for walking. Some of these are former roads between towns, while others are logging roads that were used during logging operations and then later abandoned. Forest rangers and park officials, in their efforts to accommodate a steadily increasing hiking public, and with little time on their schedules for trail-blazing, have often simply put blazes or signs on these old roads and labeled them on their maps as foot trails. But these old roads often do not pass near the most interesting natural scenery because they were originally transportation routes, following the lines of least resistance in mountainous areas. Cut trails, usually designed and cleared by local hiking clubs, make for more adventurous hiking and often involve steep climbs with considerable elevation gain. Combinations of these two types of trails, with an occasional bushwhack or roadwalk, make up the circuit hikes in this guide.

Most of the trails utilized in the 25 hikes are marked with paint blazes or markers, usually on trees, though sometimes on rocks. A single marker indicates the route of the trail. Two markers warn the hiker that a turn is imminent, and generally the upper marker is offset in the direction of the turn. In some cases — usually in state parks or forests — signs are posted indicating the name of the trail and sometimes its length as well. In areas that are not well maintained, markings can often be inconsistent or faded. Good woods sense and close attention to the text may be needed in these sections. Where trails are not marked at all, I have attempted to alert the reader to this fact and have endeavored to make the descriptive text of the route as clear as possible.

The short description that introduces each hike will hopefully alert the hiker to possible problems or complications. Although none of the hikes in this guide are very long, they may seem so to those not in the best of shape. If you are not sure of your ability, start with the easier hikes and work up to the longer ones. The hiking time given is a conservative estimate of the length of time most people will need to hike the route described. For some, the estimated time may be just right for the hike, but not long enough for leisurely rest stops. For others, the hike may not take as long as the estimated time.

The introduction to each hike also sets forth the highest and lowest elevations found along the way. Since a large elevation differential generally means a good physical workout, this information can also be a good guide to the difficulty of the hike. Where possible, I have routed hikes in such a way that steep climbs occur near the beginning of the hike, allowing for a more relaxed finish. I've also given a lot of thought to reaching interesting destinations at proportionate intervals within the hike, and I have indicated appropriate places to eat, rest and relax.

The maps that accompany each hike should allow you to determine your location along the trail. A scale in both kilometers and miles, and a north arrow (the arrow points true north) is provided with each map. The magnetic declination in northern New Jersey is about 12.5 degrees west of north (if the needle of your compass is turned to point to 347.5

degrees, the compass will be aligned properly). Hiking is not really a sport — it is more of a multifaceted activity. Hikers who might use this book range from trail runners to nature walkers, although most are somewhere in between. Good exercise, companionship, the aesthetic appreciation of nature, the study of rocks, plants and animals, photography — all these are reasons why people choose to go hiking. Whatever the reason may be that you wish to go on a hike, you will enjoy it more if you bring along the right equipment.

First on the list of essentials is footwear. Many trails climb over rocks, some scurry up loose gravel, and others are very muddy during part of the year. The wrong shoes can ruin a hike. Today's lightweight hiking boots, some with ankle collars and air-cushioned soles, are extremely comfortable and very rugged. These boots can take a dunking and have a tread that grips rock well. In warm weather, some hikers prefer good quality running shoes. In cold and wet weather, rubber-bottom boots with leather uppers and felt liners are appropriate. Under icy conditions, often found on the northern and more shaded slopes of the mountains, some type of crampon is essential. Small, four-toothed instep crampons are inexpensive and can make a slippery descent much safer. If the trail is covered with deep snow, snowshoes are appropriate, particularly those designed with bindings on an axle that facilitate climbing. Some trails described in this book are suitable for cross-country skiing if the conditions are right.

A day pack is another valuable piece of equipment for the hiker. This may be the traditional pack with shoulder straps or one of the newer lumbar packs. The pack itself need not be large, but it should be comfortable and capable of carrying some extra clothing, particularly in winter. In summer, a smaller pack may be sufficient. The pack should include a first-aid kit, a water bottle or canteen (carry water from home or purify it with a filter or iodine), a pocket knife, a map and compass, a small flashlight (in case it gets dark before you get out of the woods), a length of cord or string, rain gear of some sort, tissues or toilet paper, and some food. Additional items that you may wish to include are sunscreen, sunglasses, tampons and medications. Proper clothing for each season is a must, and a layering system is recommended in which several items are worn and taken off as needed. During the late spring, summer and early fall, be sure to bring along insect repellent. Although Lyme disease, transmitted by ticks, is not common in mountainous hiking areas, every hiker should know something about it and how to prevent it.

I have found it convenient to keep the basic items, such as the knife, compass, flashlight, etc., in a ditty bag which goes in the pack and can be taken out easily if another pack is worn. Water bottles, particularly the wide-mouthed Nalgene brand, are preferable to canteens. They come in many sizes and are unbreakable and leakproof. For rain gear, a poncho (which, when combined with that length of cord, can double as a makeshift shelter) is probably adequate, although a combination of rainjacket and rainpants offers much better protection in wind-driven rains. Although plastic ponchos or parka shells are waterproof, they are not comfortable for active hiking, as they keep moisture in as well as out. Some of the newer outdoor fabrics (such as Gore-Tex) breathe well and are more comfortable for hiking in the rain, although they are considerably more expensive.

Probably the most important thing a hiker can have is what I call good "woods sense." This is the ability to know in which compass direction you're heading, to be able to follow a vague or confusing trail, to know almost immediately when you are lost (so that you can get "unlost" without wasting time), and to correctly estimate distances. All of the above come with experience. Hikers should also know their limits and not put unnecessary strain on their bodies or on their companions. First-time hikers are encouraged to start by taking a few short hikes to get a feel for what they are capable of and comfortable with. Parents should be sensitive to their children's needs and have realistic expectations about what they are capable of. Every hiker eventually finds that he has a preference for a particular pace and particular hiking conditions, and this will influence his choice of hiking companions.

A final word on the trails themselves is appropriate here. Trails should not be taken for granted. Somebody, or some group, usually keeps them in good shape and cleans them up on a regular basis. Although a few hikes in this book utilize unmarked and unmaintained trails, I've tried to keep most of the loops on pathways that are in good shape. Please help to keep them that way. Pick up trash if you find it, and move that recently fallen branch off the trail. If you are interested in doing trail maintenance, a volunteer activity that is quite rewarding, contact the Trail Conference.

A Note on Mountain Bikes

When the first edition of this guidebook was published in 1984, mountain bikes (not to be confused with motorized dirt bikes) were non-existent. In recent years, however, the number of mountain bikes on hiking trails has increased dramatically. In certain areas, mountain bikers now often outnumber hikers. Rules regulating the use of mountain bikes on public land are still in the process of being written, as land management officials nationwide begin to take into account their increasing popularity. Consequently, hikers are now warned to expect mountain bikes on some trails mentioned in this book.

The 1990s ushered in an era of conflicts among different trail user groups. From the perspective of many hikers, mountain bikes are a menace. Few hikers enjoy the experience of having to dodge a squadron of helmeted mountain bikers charging downhill towards them on a narrow trail. Hikers walk quietly through nature, disturbing very little of it. Hiking organizations also have a long history of trail-building and maintenance. Indeed, the very existence of trails channelizes the flow of humans through natural areas and helps prevents the degradation of the environment. There is no question that heavy mountain bike use greatly degrades trails. Many popular hiking trails have grown wider and muddier since the advent of the mountain bicycle. In recent years, complaints from hikers have forced mountain bikers to acknowledge the problems their form of recreation causes, and they have begun to organize into user groups and in some cases have become involved in trail building and restoration.

Currently, some hiking areas have restrictions on mountain

bikes. For example, they are not allowed on the entire Appalachian Trail. In the opinion of this author, mountain bikes should be restricted to wide woods roads or logging lanes, carriage roads, and trails that mountain bike clubs have built themselves. Since mountain bikes tear up sensitive trail, they should not be allowed on footpaths built and maintained by the hiking community, and mountain bikers should avoid riding during especially muddy periods. These opinions are shared by many in the hiking community. As one leader of a large hiking club has said: "We don't mind mountain bikers on our trails; in fact, we invite them. We just ask that they leave their bikes at home."

In general, the hikes in this book have been designed for hikers, not mountain bikers, so one should generally meet few mountain bikes when following the hikes described in the book. In those instances where mountain bikes are likely to be encountered in the course of the hike, mention is made of this fact in the introduction to the hike.

The Geology and Early History of Northern New Jersey

Most geological accounts that attempt to explain to the general public the complex series of events which resulted in the present landscape of North Jersey are difficult to follow. There are two main reasons for this. First, geologists, like other scientists, have their own technical language and often have difficulty communicating in laymen's terms. Second, geologists are not entirely sure of the actual sequence of geologic events in New Jersey but, like most scientists, attempt to make up for this lack of certainty by offering hypotheses. While these behavior patterns may be standard operating procedure for scientists, they require the average lay reader to have a far more than casual acquaintance with geology. Thus, most accounts of the geologic history of New Jersey are probably incomprehensible to most people. As a non-geologist, I will attempt to remedy this situation in the paragraphs below as best I can. (Readers interested in reading more on the subject of New Jersey geology are referred to John McPhee's book *In Suspect Terrain.*)

To begin, New Jersey's geological history is quite complex and presents more difficulties to geologists than might be the case in some other regions of the country. Northern New Jersey features a number of extremely ancient rock formations which have been subjected to both recognizable and questionable changes for at least one billion years. There are areas where sediments, deposited over this ancient bedrock and gradually compacted into rock, were later totally eroded and washed away, leaving huge gaps in the geological history.

23

The Appalachian Mountains cut diagonally, southwest to northeast, across northern New Jersey. Built in stages, they were probably formed from the eroded rock of older mountain ranges, and interestingly they appear to be related to the mountains of Ireland, Scotland and Norway. How can this be? The "drifting continents" theory, also known as plate tectonics, suggests that Europe and North America collided, probably more than once. The slow collision of these drifting continental plates pushed up both the Appalachians and the mountains of the northwestern edge of Europe. What appear to have been possibly three mountain building episodes led to a long series of events that eventually resulted in the present landscape. Ancient mountains were worn down to level plains by wind, water and ice. At times, these plains subsided and were covered with water. Erosion from newer mountains became marine deposits. Later, these deposits were raised by powerful forces beneath the surface of the earth, leaving the newly deposited sediments at high elevations. There were also some very significant lava flows that occurred in central New Jersey late in the Triassic Era which will be described below. These were probably created by a rifting of the land as the continents pulled apart.

It is known that during certain periods of the Paleozoic and Mesozoic Eras (between 570 and 65 million years ago), the land that is today's New Jersey was subjected to folding and faulting, probably due to the collision of land masses mentioned above. In some places, the land was compressed like a rug pushed together from both ends. The cross-section of Kittatinny Mountain at the Delaware Water Gap illustrates graphically how layers once formed on lake and sea bottoms are no longer horizontal. But these ancient layered and compressed mountainous surfaces were eventually worn down to a plain.

A peneplain is a nearly level surface — which in our case dips (is tilted) just slightly to the east and the sea. This was New Jersey's landscape about 65 million years ago, at the beginning of the Cenozoic Era (just after the dinosaurs disappeared). The part of the plain that is now High Point State Park was slightly higher by about a few hundred feet than what are now the Highlands, and this area in turn was a few hundred feet higher than what are now the Watchungs. In fact, the tops of these mountain ridges today constitute the remaining surface of what is called the Schooley Peneplain, the rest of the surface having been worn away. When the Schooley Peneplain was uplifted — that is, when the land actually rose uniformly to its present position above sea level — the down-cutting action of streams and rivers began to remove the softer material, leaving the more resistant rocks as mountains.

The concept of the Schooley Peneplain is a useful to bear in mind when considering the appearance of the North Jersey landscape. For example, consider the vista from the overlooks on Interstate Route 80 in Allamuchy Mountain State Park. The view northwest out to the Kittatinny range is a spectacular one, with farmland in the foreground and the Kittatinny ridge line in the distance. What we see from here is an almost even ridge line, a constant elevation broken only by an occasional gap, the most dramatic being the Delaware Water Gap. To the northeast, the ridge line dips slightly near Catfish Pond and again at Culvers Gap, through which U.S. Route 206 passes.

Now climb, or more likely drive, to Sunrise Mountain in Stokes State Forest and look out towards the Highlands to the east. What you will see is a relatively flat-topped plateau from north to south. Because of the width of the province, there are no significant breaks. Only a few east-west gaps occur because of cutting by rivers, such as the Pequannock and the Rockaway, but their effects do not change the perspective from this viewpoint on the Kittatinny ridge. Again, when viewed from a distance, the mountain tops appear to be level.

Next, climb to the outlook on Mt. Kemble in Jockey Hollow (or look at the skyline from I-80 eastbound near Parsippany and the junction with I-280) and take a look at the Watchung ridge to the east. It's the same thing — flat-topped ridges with a few low gaps. These three summit areas become progressively lower in elevation as one moves eastward, preserving the original dip of the old Schooley Peneplain. The top of the Palisades ridge completes this portion of the original plain and, as would be expected, the Palisades average about 200 feet lower in elevation than the Watchungs.

The three distinct mountainous regions described above are (from east to west) classified by geologists as the Piedmont Lowlands, the Highlands, and the Ridge and Valley Province. We have utilized this natural division in organizing the hikes in this guide. Each region has its own unique properties and history, as we will see in the following sections.

The Piedmont Lowlands

In this easternmost province, the bedrock consists of the usually red and crumbly Brunswick and Newark Shales, which break easily and can be excavated rapidly. It is no coincidence that incredible rates of building construction occur in this province, since the land is easily moved around. We will encounter this shale, which was deposited as silt during the Triassic Era (200 million years ago), in parts of the Watchungs where it has not been totally washed out.

The chief feature for hikers in the Piedmont Lowlands Province is the Watchung Mountains, which range in elevation from 400 to 600 feet above sea level. The name of this range is derived from the Indian name for the land around these high hills. The Watchungs, like the Palisades, originated as magma (molten rock) that penetrated the surrounding tilted layers of rock (shales and sandstones). When viewed from the east, they rise abruptly from the plain. The Watchungs reached the surface as lava flows and cooled rather rapidly, forming basalt. Near Jockey Hollow, these flows made contact with the Highlands bedrock. The magma of the Palisades sill (a sill is an igneous intrusion) did not reach the surface and cooled very slowly, leaving larger crystals in the rock and some rather long and spectacular six-sided vertical columns — hence the name Palisades. The rock of the Palisades is called diabase. Both the Watchungs and the Palisades have been extensively quarried for road paving material.

The Watchungs formed a natural barrier to progress from the east and have proven to be a major deterrent to at least two invasions. In the Revolutionary War, the invasion of the

British was halted by these hills, which presented no small barrier to them. Washington kept his troops at Jockey Hollow, safely west of the easternmost Watchung range, and when the British attempted to break through these natural ramparts at the pass near Millburn and Springfield, they were pushed back to the flatter, lower-lying areas. A second invasion, continuing to this day, is the one led by developers and building contractors. Difficulties in both building (due to the ruggedness of the Watchung and Highlands bedrock) and transportation (because of the lack of easy passes) had until recently slowed development in the central and western sections of the state. If it were not for the natural wall formed by the Watchungs, this book might consist primarily of urban and suburban circuit hikes.

Two gaps in the curving wall of the Watchungs are worth a closer look. At the Millburn-Springfield gap, mentioned above for its role in the Revolutionary War, the ancient Passaic River made its way to the sea. The gap was probably a rocky gorge which became gradually steeper due to the steady rising of the land surface. Remember that the entire New Jersey area was once a smooth, tilted plain, with established drainage patterns. With the rising of the plain, these established drainage patterns began to cut deeper into the ground. As the land rose, the ancient Passaic River found itself cutting through the erosion-resistant trap rock (basalt) of the Watchung ridge — which was just beginning to become an imposing ridge because of this differential erosion. During the Ice Age, this gap at Millburn-Springfield became blocked with glacial debris, and a dam was formed. The interior lowland between the Watchung ridge and the Highlands Province, which was mostly Brunswick shales and had been steadily wearing down, became filled with water, forming what is known by geologists as glacial Lake

Passaic. This very large lake (maximum dimensions were thirty miles by ten miles) found its drainage at a second and larger gap in the Watchungs near Paterson and Little Falls. The present Great Falls of Paterson testifies to the difficulties the river has had in cutting through the Watchung ridge. The only remnants of glacial Lake Passaic are the Great Swamp, which offers some interesting hiking possibilities (see Hike #2), and the Great Piece Meadows, which can be seen from Interstate Route 80, between N.J. Route 23 and Interstate Route 287.

The Watchungs, in the area near Paterson, were originally settled by the Lenni Lenape, their name meaning "original people." These Native Americans were part of the Algonkian nation and had migrated to New Jersey only a few hundred years before colonial activity began. The Lenni Lenape were a peaceful people, noted for their fine stone carvings, who established settlements along the Delaware River, in the Highlands near present-day Pompton Plains, and at Tom's Point in the Great Piece Meadows. During the summer, they would journey to the ocean, where they would feast on clams and oysters. One of the original trails in New Jersey — which ran from the Delaware River near High Point to Shrewsbury Inlet near Red Bank on the Jersey coast — was used by the Lenni Lenape for this purpose. During the fall, a deer hunt was held on Garrett Mountain, the section of the Watchung ridge just south of Paterson. Men would form a long line and drive the deer north towards the peak of the mountain and the falls, where they would then be harvested.

The Highlands

Hiking can be challenging in this province, with its many ups and downs. For the most part, the province is composed of ancient Precambrian (older than 600 million years) gneiss and granite which reveal the existence of a very ancient mountain range in this area. According to some sources, these Highlands are the stumps of a range that may at one time have exceeded 10,000 feet in elevation. Downcutting action by streams and rivers has provided much vertical relief in this province, making it quite rugged in places. The province extends from the New York state line, where it is known as the Hudson Highlands, to the Pennsylvania border. The entire province is known as the New England Upland, the New Jersey section being part of a southern spur. The elevations — up to 1,460 feet — are among the highest in the northern part of the state. The highest elevations are near the edge of the Ridge and Valley Province, which would be expected, given the characteristics of the original Schooley Peneplain.

In the northeastern part of the province are the Ramapo Mountains, which form a striking escarpment, both physically and on topographic maps. While the elevations are not much over 1,000 feet here, the relief is substantial, and it is relief that counts most in establishing a mountainous area's ruggedness. For example, the relief from valley floor to the high summits in Rocky Mountain National Park is similar to that of the White Mountains of New Hampshire.

South of the Ramapos, the eastern flank of the Highlands becomes less sharply defined, and near the Boonton-Morristown area it fractures into a series of somewhat isolated ridges called the Passaic Mountains. A good view of this range can be had from the westbound lanes of U.S. Route 46 at Great Notch near Little Falls. Even farther south, the topography becomes decidedly less rugged until the Delaware River is reached, where the relief is caused by the cutting action of the river.

The Lenni Lenape had a number of settlements in this section of the Highlands. One of their largest villages was at Pompton Plains, just below the western hills. From these low-lying villages, hunting parties would enter the surrounding mountains and set up temporary camps. Natural rock overhangs located near a water source were utilized for such purposes, and a number of these have yielded projectile points. One of these was Bear Rock, located below Pyramid Mountain (see Hike #6).

A number of the original Indian paths have become major roadways. U.S. Route 202, from Oakland to Suffern, along the edge of the Ramapos, began as a trail, and so did parts of N.J. Route 23 near Pompton and N.J. Route 10 from Dover to Newark. These are all lowland routes which follow rivers and utilize passes between ridges; they are not the skyline routes preferred by today's hikers.

In the northern part of the Highlands, extensive tracts of land have been set aside for conservation and public use. Hiking trails abound, and the region offers excellent hiking opportunities. The summits of the many ridges here are similar to those found in New York's Harriman and Bear Mountain State Parks, which are an extension of the same range. Many summits are bare rock strewn with boulders, with a few pitch pines struggling for existence. Extensive views are common from these unique summits and rock outcrops. This type of

summit does not occur further to the south in this province because glaciation — which was responsible for the removal of any prior accumulation of sediments and soil — did not extend very far south of the line of Interstate Route 80.

Typical evidence of glacial activity in the northern Highlands is seen in bare rock exposures with glacial striations or grooves cut into the bedrock by the glacially driven rocks that were picked up along the way. Glacial chattermarks, which are gouges caused by the "bouncing" of stones pushed along by the ice sheet, are common, and so are glacial "erratics," or loose boulders deposited on summits as the ice melted. Some glacial erratics are found perched on smaller rocks. Geologists explain this as the result of a large rock settling onto smaller ones as the glacial ice melted. Later, most of the underlying debris was washed out, leaving several small rocks propping up the boulder. There are, however, a few cases where such propped-up rocks appear to form patterns that align with significant astronomical directions, and it is possible that early inhabitants of the region reorganized some of these erratics for ceremonial or timekeeping purposes (see Hike #6).

Norvin Green State Forest, the Ramapos, the Sterling Ridge and Wawayanda State Park are all good places to explore the rounded summits and steep escarpments characteristic of this province. Bearfort Mountain (Hike #11), which lies in the central portion of the Highlands just west of Greenwood Lake, is of particular interest. While its summit ridge is as high in elevation as the surrounding ridges, it is composed of a completely different kind of rock, much younger and strikingly dissimilar in composition from the gray Precambrian gneiss of the Highlands. Bearfort Mountain is an anomaly in the midst of the Highlands. It is more closely related to the

Paleozoic strata of the Ridge and Valley Province (Kittatinny Mountain), yet it is miles to the east and in the midst of another geological formation. It appears that the Bearfort Ridge began during Paleozoic times as a long bed of sediments laid down in what may have been an inland sea or sound in the midst of the Highlands. After folding and faulting, the strata was upturned, and it has proven to be highly resistant to weathering. The result is variety in the northern Highlands area, with Bearfort Mountain offering a different base rock (a conglomerate made up of white quartz pebbles in a puddingstone matrix) and a long ridge line much like Kittatinny Mountain.

In the central and southern portion of the Highlands are several areas of public land worth exploring, but these are fewer in number than in the north due to development and agricultural uses. The terrain in this section, which did not suffer the effects of the last Ice Age, tends to be less rocky, and as a result there is more farmland. Hacklebarney State Park and Jockey Hollow are good examples of unglaciated Highlands topography.

The large veins of high-quality iron ore found in the ancient Precambrian rock of the New Jersey and Hudson Highlands were the source of an active iron-mining industry. In the region covered in this guide, the hiker will occasionally come upon some remnant of this activity which shaped the economy and the land itself for over one hundred years. The mines themselves can be located, although most are filled in. In Norvin Green State Forest (Hike #9) there are two easily accessible mines. Blue Mine, although flooded, presents an interesting spectacle. Even more fascinating is the Roomy Mine — located nearby on the yellow-blazed Mine Trail — which penetrates the hill for about a hundred feet.

There are a few furnaces still standing in this region. These are always found near swift-running streams, since it was necessary to have a water wheel operate the bellows to keep the smelting fire hot. The Long Pond Iron Works, near the start of the Sterling Ridge Trail in Hewitt, which features remains of the wheels and furnace, is worth a visit. The Wawayanda Furnace (Hike #15) is easily accessible and is in relatively good shape for such an old structure. Farther to the south stand the remains of the Clinton Furnace, on Clinton Road just south of the falls. When operating, the furnaces were fired with charcoal produced from the slow burning of logs in pits covered by earth. Once the furnaces were fired, they were kept going for long periods. Separated from the ore with the help of limestone, the iron would trickle out to be cast into pigs.

The iron industry in New Jersey had important political consequences during the Revolutionary War. Robert Erskine, who took over the Ringwood mines after the first ironmaster (Peter Hasenclever) was relieved of his duties, sided with Washington and used his forges to make iron products for the Continental Army. He also became surveyor-general for Washington and made many important and accurate maps. The iron industry in the colonies suffered from British laws prohibiting the manufacture of any finished items in the colonies themselves. All iron made had to be shipped in pigs to England, where it was worked into items to be sold back to the colonists. This was as aggravating as the tea tax, so it is understandable that the iron industry sided with the rebels.

The Ridge and Valley Province

It is in this province that the highest elevations in the state are attained. The long and narrow Kittatinny Mountain ridge stretching from the Delaware Water Gap to the New York state line averages about 1,500 feet in height, but rises to 1,803 feet at High Point. The Kittatinny Ridge is composed of dipping Silurian sandstones and conglomerates, about 420 million years old and white in color. A number of cliffs are found at the edge of the eastern escarpment, which has a steep slope throughout its entire length.

Kittatinny Mountain is just a small part of a long series of ridges which extend from New York State southward. In New York, the extension of Kittatinny Mountain is known as the Shawangunk Mountains, which attain elevations of over 2,000 feet. This area contains a number of high cliffs, regarded by many as the best in the east for rock climbing. To the southwest of Kittatinny Mountain, the ridge continues through Pennsylvania as Blue Mountain. Paralleling this long ridge to the east is a broad lowland, in New Jersey known as the Kittatinny Valley, hence the name "Ridge and Valley Province." This is a valley of rich farmland and low, gentle hills. When viewed from the ridge, this valley reveals a New Jersey worthy of the name Garden State.

The long, narrow and very distinctive shape of Kittatinny Mountain is used annually for navigation by soaring birds in their southward migration. In autumn, at various places along the ridge, birders congregate to observe hawks and other birds. One of New Jersey's major bird monitoring stations is located near Blue Mountain (Hike #22), and many birders gather along what is called "Raccoon Ridge" near Mt. Mohican (see Hike #24).

Probably the most spectacular section of the Ridge and Valley Province is at the Delaware Water Gap. Here, the Delaware River — on its way to the sea — has cut an impressive notch in the ridge which rises over 1,000 feet above sea level. Again, this illustrates what happened when the ancient drainage patterns of the Schooley Peneplain were disrupted by uplifting. A second notable gap is Culvers Gap, the notch in the ridge through which U.S. Route 206 passes. This gap may have been a result of an earlier route of the ancient Delaware River or one of its tributaries — a route which failed to cut faster than the land was uplifted. It is probable that the success of the cut through the ridge at the Delaware Water Gap is due to the weakness of the ridge at that point.

Mt. Minsi, the peak on the Pennsylvania side of the Delaware Water Gap, was named for the Minsi tribe of the Lenni Lenape, which lived in the mountainous sections of northern New Jersey. Mt. Tammany on the New Jersey side was named for Lenni Lenape Chief Tamenund. There were once a number of Indian villages along the Delaware River, including one large settlement on Minisink Island near High Point. One of their legacies is the Old Mine Road, originally a trail that extended north from the Delaware Water Gap area all the way to Kingston, N.Y. The Pahaquarry copper mines, located near the Delaware Water Gap, were the site of explorations by the Dutch in the 1600s.

Today, nearly all of the Kittatinny Ridge is protected either by the New Jersey Department of Environmental Protection (High Point State Park and Stokes and Worthington State Forests) or by the United States Department of the Interior, National Park Service, which is the steward of the Delaware Water Gap National Recreation Area. The area attracts thousands (if not millions) of people annually, yet most visitors never go far from the road. There are still large stretches of wilderness along the ridge offering hikers steep climbs, scenic vistas, and the opportunity to escape into the wilderness.

The Piedmont Lowlands

1

Watchung Reservation

General Description: A long, winding, moderately strenuous, up-and-down hike, with frequent trail intersections requiring attention to trail markers.
Type of Trail: Footpaths and bridle paths.
Distance: 8.5 miles
Hiking Time: 5 hours
Lowest Elevation: 220 feet
Highest Elevation: 540 feet
USGS Quad: Chatham, Roselle
Other Maps: Union County Department of Parks and Recreation map

Watchung Reservation, like South Mountain Reservation north of it, straddles the first and second Watchung ridges. It is a suburban park, riddled with dirt roads, bridle paths and picnic areas, and quite heavily used, especially on weekends. Not only is the park located in the heart of a heavily populated residential area, but it is constantly subject to noise pollution from the adjacent I-78. Nevertheless, the park has many interesting features, and for most of the hike you are out of the sight of civilization. Mountain bikes are not permitted in the park, but you may come into contact with horses, which are allowed on designated bridle paths.

This hike mainly follows the Sierra Trail — blazed by a local chapter of the Sierra Club in the early 1980s — which winds around the park, passing through most of the more scenic and interesting sections. It follows a combination of bridle paths and footpaths and is marked with white squares. (Originally, the trail was marked with white X's, and some of these markings are still visible.) You can get a good workout doing this trail, but you will have to pay close attention to the blazes, as there are numerous intersections with other trails. The main hike described below is recommended for those with good trail sense, good map-reading skills and reasonable physical stamina. Others may wish to try the short hike of 1.5 miles, which begins from the same trailhead.

Trailhead: Take Interstate 78 east to Exit 44 (New Providence, Berkeley Heights). At the traffic light, turn left onto Glenside Avenue. After 1.2 miles, turn right onto Tracy Drive (County Route 645) and enter the Reservation. You will pass Lake Surprise and some picnic areas. When you reach the traffic circle, make a right onto Summit Lane, and then right onto New Providence Road. The parking area is to the right where the road makes a sharp turn to the left. The Trailside Nature and Science Center is located a few hundred feet north of this parking area.

*If you are proceeding west on Interstate 78, take Exit 43 (New Providence, Berkeley Heights). Turn right at the first light onto McMane Avenue. When you reach a **T** intersection with Glenside Avenue, turn left and follow the directions above.*

Directions: Before beginning your hike, obtain a trail map of the Reservation from a box near the parking area or from the Trailside Nature and Science Center. Start the hike at the trailhead — on the extension of New Providence Road, across from the southwest corner of the parking area — indicated by a large wooden sign that reads "Nature Trail."

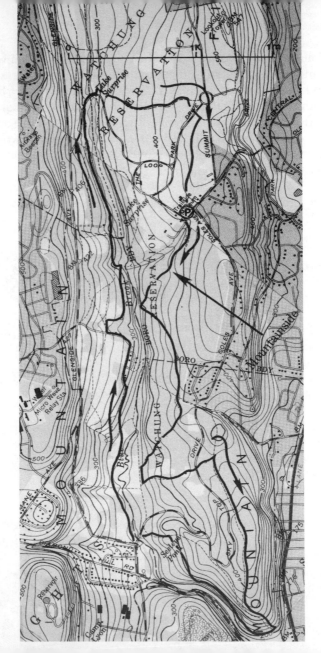

Follow the white markers of the Sierra Trail across the brook and then downhill alongside a small glen. For the first three-quarters of a mile, you will also be following the route of some of the nature trails. At first, the white blazes run concurrently with the Green Trail. Before reaching a wide bridge, they turn left and run briefly with the Yellow Trail, then turn right and begin to parallel a very scenic gorge to the left. The Blue Trail soon joins, and the path begins to descend.

At the end of the gorge, the trail route approaches Blue Brook, the main watercourse between the first and second Watchungs. Here the Blue Trail leaves to the right. You should follow the white-blazed Sierra Trail as it turns left and briefly follows the brook. The trail soon bears left and climbs away from the brook, bears left again at the next intersection, then turns right at the following junction. In another quarter of a mile, the trail crosses a small brook (which may be dry). Be careful to proceed straight ahead here and then bear left, uphill. (The trail leading downhill to the right has some old white blazes, but that is not the correct route.) After passing some houses to the left, the trail crosses a dirt road and soon begins a gradual descent.

About two miles from the start, the white blazes turn left onto a dirt road. The trail follows the dirt road for only 300 feet, and then turns left, leaving the road and continuing on a footpath. (Be sure to look for this turn.) It ascends through a beautiful pine forest, planted by the CCC in the 1930s, and soon reaches an open grassy area, with a picnic pavilion ahead. Bear right here and follow a cinder road out to the paved Sky Top Drive. The trail crosses the road and re-enters the woods, then makes a sharp right turn onto a wide woods road parallel to Sky Top Drive (which often may be seen to the right). About three-quarters of a mile from the crossing of the paved road, the trail begins to descend. As the trail bends to the left, a short path to the right leads to an overlook above an abandoned quarry, with I-78 visible in the distance.

After descending more steeply, the trail makes a sharp right turn in sight of Route 22 and follows an eroded gully (with a number of blowdowns) down to Green Brook. It runs along the brook, with New Providence Road on the other side. In about a third of a mile, you will reach the site of an old mill, with many brick and concrete ruins still visible. After passing the ruins of the stone dam that supplied power to the mill, the trail bears right and climbs steeply to an overlook, then descends and once more reaches Sky Top Drive, about 4.5 miles from the start of the hike.

The Sierra Trail turns left and follows the road, using the highway bridge to cross Blue Brook, with Seeley's Pond to the left. After crossing the bridge, the trail immediately turns right, goes through a grassy area, and re-enters the woods. It follows a footpath through dense vegetation and crosses several small brooks on a wooden boardwalk. Just beyond, the trail turns left onto the Drake Farm Road, then turns right, leaving the road and continues on a footpath. In another third of a mile, the trail turns left onto a wide dirt road and finally emerges on a paved road at the Deserted Village of Feltville. Named for David Felt, a New York City businessman who founded the village in 1845 to house the workers at his nearby paper mill, it was abandoned about thirty years later, and then converted into a summer resort known as Glenside Park, which thrived until 1916. It was purchased by the Union County Park Commission in the 1920s, and some of the buildings in the area are now being restored.

The Sierra Trail follows the paved road through the village

for 0.4 mile. After passing the general store — now being restored as an interpretive center for the village — and an adjacent home, the Sierra Trail turns right on a bridle path. In 200 feet, it turns right again onto a wide path, and soon passes a small cemetery which contains the grave markers of the Willcocks and Badgley families, who first settled the area in 1736. The path soon narrows. About a third of a mile from the cemetery, the white-blazed trail turns right, descends on a bridle path for 400 feet, then turns left, leaving the bridle path, and immediately bears right onto a footpath. Soon, the trail reaches the stone dam of Lake Surprise, built in 1845 to provide power for David Felt's paper mill. The trail continues along the northwestern shore of this long but narrow lake for almost a mile, then turns right at paved Tracy Drive, crossing the lake on a bridge. On the other side of the bridge, the white blazes turn left, crossing the road. From here, we

General Store of the Deserted Village of Feltville

will use only portions of the Sierra Trail on the way back to the parking area.

After crossing Tracy Drive, follow the white blazes for 100 feet and turn right onto a bridle path that immediately crosses an entrance road to the stables. For a few hundred feet, Tracy Drive will be visible on your right. In about 300 yards, the white-blazed Sierra Trail will rejoin the bridle path. Continue ahead, following the white markers, for the next 0.4 mile, but do not turn left where they leave the path near the traffic circle; instead, bear right, following the wide path across the paved road. In 300 feet, you will meet the Sierra Trail again; this time, leave the bridle path and follow the white blazes to the right, onto a footpath. Continue ahead on the white-blazed trail, which eventually is joined by the Red Trail. In about half a mile, the trail will pass the Trailside Nature and Science Center and reach the parking area where you started the hike.

Short Hike: From the trailhead, take the white-blazed Sierra Trail (which shares the route with the Green, Yellow and Blue Trails for a while), following the first two paragraphs of the above description of the longer hike. When you approach Blue Brook at the end of the gorge, turn right, following the Blue Trail. This path is level and heads north, paralleling Blue Brook. After crossing a bridge, continue to follow the blue markers as they turn right, now heading uphill. In about 500 feet, you will reach a junction with the Orange Trail. Continue straight ahead, now following the orange blazes, and you will soon reach a road just below the Trailside Museum. Walk along the road a few hundred feet to your car.

2 | The Great Swamp Lord Stirling Park

> **General Description:** Easy walk through lowland forest, alongside a river, and over swampland on boardwalks.
> **Type of Trail:** Wide grassy footpaths and boardwalks.
> **Distance:** 3.5 miles
> **Hiking Time:** 2 hours
> **Elevation:** constant 220 feet
> **USGS Quad:** Bernardsville
> **Other Maps:** Somerset County Park Commission map

The Great Swamp is a remnant of glacial Lake Passaic, an immense body of water once contained within the walls of the Watchung Mountains. Today, much of this extensive wetland is public land, with portions under the jurisdiction of the Morris and Somerset County park systems, and a large part included in the Great Swamp National Wildlife Refuge, administered by the National Park Service. The Great Swamp is quite wild and is home to many birds and mammals. It is not unusual to spot hawks, fox, deer and many water birds during the course of a short walk. For the hiker, Lord Stirling Park near Basking Ridge offers a variety of trails and boardwalks that penetrate woodland, river and swamp. This Somerset County park, named for the original landowner who aspired to a high title of nobility, is the location of a county Environmental Education Center.

Trailhead: Take Interstate Route 287 to Exit 26A (Basking Ridge) and get onto North Maple Avenue. Drive 2.5 miles, bearing left onto South Maple Avenue as you near the town, and make a left onto Lord Stirling Road. Continue for another mile to the Environmental Education Center, and park in its large parking lot. Before beginning your hike, sign in and pick up a free trail map at the center.

The trailhead may also be reached via NJ Transit, which provides frequent rail service from Hoboken (with connections from New York Penn Station) to the Millington and Lyons stations on the Gladstone Line. However, both of these stations are some distance from the trailhead, necessitating a roadwalk of over two miles along pleasant semi-rural roads.

Directions: The hike described below utilizes portions of wide paths and boardwalks. Some of the trails are marked,

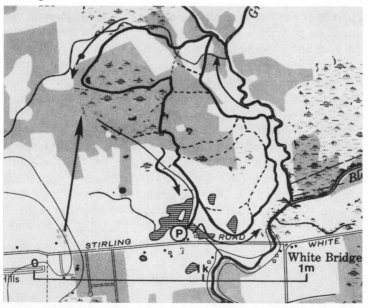

but the markings are rather sparse. However, if you pick up a copy of the very detailed trail map available at the Environmental Education Center and follow it carefully, you should always know exactly where you are. Even if you get confused as to your bearings, you will not be lost for long, as each trail intersection is posted with a sign indicating the direction back to the center. For most of the hike, you will be making right turns at each intersection. A significant portion of the walking is through fields and swamps open to the sky — very different from the usual wooded corridors typical of North Jersey hiking. Over a mile of the hike is on boardwalks, but some portions of the non-boardwalk sections may be muddy during wet periods.

From the parking area, walk to the right of the main building along a wide crushed-stone path, with Branta Pond to your left. When you reach the end of the pond, make a sharp right, heading almost back the way you came, on a grassy lane marked with a yellow reflector on a stake. Keep to the right at the first intersection. After passing Esox Pond to the right, make a right at the next trail junction and then immediately bear left, still following the yellow stakes. On the left is the East Observation Blind, which overlooks swampy Lily Pad Pond. Just ahead, after the trail enters the woods, turn right onto another path that heads east, with the yellow stakes again pointing you in the correct direction. The trail soon approaches the Passaic River and then turns north, paralleling the west bank of the river.

After approaching the river once more and crossing the June Beetle Bridge, the trail curves left, away from the river. At the next intersection, turn right and then immediately bear right again onto a path that goes along the edge of a meadow. In 500 feet, a boardwalk to the right leads to the East

Observation Tower, which offers a view over the tiny river and well beyond. It is well worth the short detour. After enjoying the view, return to the trail and turn right, following the wide, grassy path along the edge of the meadow, and keeping the woods to your right. At the end of the meadow, bear right at a **Y** intersection. In another 200 feet, a boardwalk leaves to the left, but you should continue straight ahead, now following dark orange markers.

After continuing for another quarter of a mile through a wooded area, the trail begins to follow a long stretch of boardwalk. At the next intersection, bear right and continue along the boardwalk as it meanders through the East Marsh, a swampy area with a number of trees. At one point, the boardwalk approaches the Passaic River, with a short spur leading out to a viewpoint over the river. A sign informs you that across the river is the Great Swamp National Wildlife Refuge. You are now about halfway through the hike, and you may wish to pause for a few minutes at this peaceful, quiet spot. When you are sufficiently rested, return to the main boardwalk and bear right.

At the next intersection, bear right onto an 0.7-mile-long loop, nicknamed the "Boondocks Boardwalk" after the isolated area that it goes through. Soon you will enter a large section of very wet swampland known as "La Plus Grande" — the most interesting section of wetlands in the park. After leaving the deep swamp and traversing a long section through woodland, you will come to a triangular junction of boardwalk. Again, bear right, now heading south. Do not turn right at the next junction, but continue straight ahead. Soon, the boardwalk ends, and you will continue ahead on a trail, now marked with red blazes.

In another 100 feet, you will reach a **T** intersection. Turn left, continuing to follow the red blazes, which will lead you all the way back to the Environmental Education Center (EEC). You should bear right at the next two intersections, and then make a left followed by a right. Now that you are heading back to the center, you can simply follow the ubiquitous "To EEC" signs, which you have seen at every intersection along the trail. After crossing the Backswimmer and Aphid Bridges and going around a bend in the trail, the Environmental Education Center will be visible ahead. Bear right at the next intersection onto the path on which you began the hike, and proceed back to the center and the parking lot.

Boardwalk through La Plus Grande

3 South Mountain Reservation

General Description: A moderate hike along the main Watchung ridge on a footpath, returning along a stream.
Type of Trail: Footpaths, woods roads and bridle paths.
Distance: 6.2 miles
Hiking Time: 3-4 hours
Lowest Elevation: 200 feet
Highest Elevation: 520 feet
USGS Quad: Caldwell, Roselle
Other Maps: Essex County Department of Parks map

You will find some, but not much, quiet wilderness in the relatively large chunk of the Watchung Ridge that makes up the 2,048-acre South Mountain Reservation. Although the Reservation provides some very interesting walking possibilities, you can only temporarily escape the sounds — and even sights — of motor traffic. Constant airplane activity in the area adds to this roar. Even within the Reservation, mountain bikers may interfere with any effort to escape from the tension of population-packed New Jersey.

Nevertheless, South Mountain Reservation is one of the last remaining undeveloped sections of the Watchung ridge. The Reservation is large enough to provide a good workout, and it illustrates well some of the geology discussed earlier. There is much to see here, and it is nearby for many people. It is also readily accessible by public transportation. Indeed, it is

the only hike in this book that is reachable directly by train
— NJ Transit provides frequent service to the Millburn station from Penn Station in New York and from Hoboken.
Hemlock Falls is a first-rate waterfall for New Jersey, even
though the area around it is developed, and the views out to
the south and east and over the New York City skyline are
impressive. For the most part, this hike follows footpaths and
traverses the wildest sections of the park. The first leg of the
hike is on the yellow-blazed Lenape Trail, named for North
Jersey's Native Americans and part of a much larger trail
project that will link parklands from Newark to Millburn. Off
season, especially the winter, may be the best time to explore
the Reservation. Even though mountain bikes are not
allowed on the hiking trails, the regulations are not strictly
enforced, and you are likely to encounter mountain bikes at
some point on the hike.

Trailhead: From Route 24, follow signs to Millburn and proceed
to the Millburn railroad station (near the Paper Mill Playhouse).
The trailhead is at the Locust Grove parking area, on the north side
of Glen Avenue, just east of its intersection with Lackawanna
Place. If you are arriving by NJ Transit train, head to the northwest
corner of the station parking lot (where the Millburn First Aid
Squad is located), cross Glen Avenue, and walk up the short access
road to the Locust Grove parking area.

Directions: From the northeastern end of the parking area in
Locust Grove, follow the painted yellow blazes of the Lenape
Trail along a woods road through the picnic area, and turn
left onto a wide path leading uphill. The trail climbs steadily
on this path, bearing right at two junctions, and joining a
woods road. After about half a mile, as you reach the top of
the climb, the yellow blazes make a sharp left turn off the
road, cut through the woods on a footpath, and turn left onto

Crest Drive, a paved road which is now closed to automobile traffic (but open to bicycles). In about 500 feet, the road reaches Washington Rock, the best viewpoint in the Reservation.

A number of benches have been placed in the vicinity of this overlook, inviting the hiker to stop and take time to appreciate the beautiful vista. To the east, the New York City skyline may be seen, with the towers of the Verazzano Narrows Bridge in the distance. To the south, the view is over Millburn and Springfield, which lie in the pass through which the ancient Passaic River once flowed. Today, I-78 traffic flows through it. This is also the pass that the British attempted to use in their ill-fated march on Washington's encampment near Morristown. A commemorative plaque, with many interesting details about the Battle of Springfield, was placed here on a boulder in 1934 and rededicated in 1992.

To continue on the hike, follow the yellow markers as they descend along a paved path from the end of the stone retaining wall. To the left, you will pass a concrete overlook veranda, with stone pillars that date back to 1908. The train tracks on which you may have arrived are visible below to your right, and the Watchung Reservation, where the ridge once again rises up, is to the southwest.

Continue on the yellow-blazed Lenape Trail, now heading west. The trail soon descends and passes above an old traprock (basalt) quarry on the left. An unmarked path leads to the edge of the cliff overlooking the quarry, with a chain-link fence along the edge of the precipitous drop. Soon afterwards, the trail crosses a bridle path and enters a more remote section of the Reservation. During wet periods, you

may encounter some mud on this section, made worse by mountain bike traffic. However, this is also the most secluded stretch of trail on the hike, and it has much to offer. Two cascades tumble across the trail, although they are often dry during the summer. The first, Maple Falls Cascade, is a thin stream which plunges down a 25-foot sluiceway of exposed basalt. You'll have to leave the trail and go down a short distance for the best views. Three-quarters of a mile further on, you'll reach Beech Brook Cascade, a more modest series of falls at the point where two brooks converge.

After crossing another bridle path, the trail climbs to a high spot on the ridge, known as Mines Point. These "mines" are actually prospectors' holes dug in the late 1700s in search for copper ore, and many of them are still visible. From here, the trail levels off and, in another half a mile, reaches Ball's Bluff, named after Philander Ball, who sold the adjacent land to the Essex County Park Commission in 1896. Here, to the left of the trail, are some old stone pillars, the remnants of a picnic shelter originally built in 1908 and improved by the CCC in the 1930s. The trail now descends and crosses a bridle path. Soon, the trail begins to parallel a stream and then crosses the stream.

About 300 feet after the stream crossing, the trail comes out on a wide woods road. The yellow blazes turn left and follow the road, but you should continue straight ahead, crossing the road. You will find a distinct footpath on the other side, with blacked-out blazes. Follow this footpath for about 500 feet to a junction with another woods road, and turn left. Soon you will come to a bluff, with a stream directly ahead. Bear right and descend rather steeply, then follow the stream for another 200 feet to the base of Hemlock Falls.

This scenic waterfall is very close to South Orange Avenue, and it is a favorite hangout for local people. But it's located in a relatively quiet spot, and it's a good place to take a break and enjoy the surroundings. At the base of the falls, a pedestrian footbridge crosses the stream and leads to the top of the falls. After you've explored this interesting area and rested for a while, continue the hike by proceeding west, following the blue blazes along the woods road which parallels the north side of the stream. In 300 feet, turn sharply left, still following the blue-blazed trail (although the blazes may be hard to find at this point). In a few minutes, you will reach an intersecting woods road. Here, three blue blazes indicate the terminus of the blue trail.

Continue straight ahead, now following the white blazes of the Rahway Trail, which you will follow all the way back to Millburn. The white trail bears right and soon reaches South Orange Avenue, where it turns left and crosses the Rahway River on the highway bridge. Be careful here, as the sidewalk is rather narrow, and the vehicular traffic comes by at a high rate of speed! At the end of the guardrail, the white blazes turn sharply left, reentering the woods, and soon bear left onto a footpath which parallels the river.

After a short distance, the trail begins to ascend, and it continues along the side of a hill, with the river below to the left. This is a very beautiful section of trail, and the road is now far enough away that it is relatively quiet. About 0.6 mile from South Orange Avenue, the trail descends to river level and turns left on a woods road. After crossing a bridge over the river, it immediately bears right and follows a footpath parallel to the river.

For the remainder of the hike, you will follow the white trail as it meanders between a bridle path to the left and the Rahway River to the right. Occasionally, the trail will join the road briefly. There are places where the trail may be poorly marked or obscured by blowdowns. But it's hard to get lost if you remember to keep the river to the right and the bridle path to the left. Alternatively, you can simply follow the bridle path all the way back to Millburn, keeping right at all intersections.

Along the way, the river is punctuated by several small dams and ponds, remnants of the paper mills which once flourished in the area. About 1.3 miles from South Orange Avenue, you will note that Brookside Drive, which has paralleled the trail to the right but in the distance, begins to run directly along the west side of the river. For the rest of the way to Millburn, you will hear the constant roar of traffic along this heavily-traveled road. Soon you will pass through a dense stand of rhododendron, planted early in this century as part of a restoration project for the Reservation. From here, it is a little over a mile back to the Locust Grove parking area, where the hike began.

4 High Mountain

> **General Description:** Moderate — a stiff climb, a great view and a long walk through the woods back to your car. The route utilizes woods roads that have suffered from ATV abuse.
> **Type of Trail:** Mostly woods roads.
> **Distance:** 4 miles
> **Hiking Time:** 2.5 hours
> **Lowest Elevation:** 500 feet
> **Highest Elevation:** 885 feet
> **USGS Quad:** Paterson
> **Other Maps:** Wayne Township High Mountain trail map

North of where the Passaic River cuts through the Watchung ridge at Paterson is the Preakness Range. Among the several summits here, *High Mountain* — the highest mountain in view of the ocean on the east coast south of Maine — offers the hiker outstanding views and a good workout. High Mountain has a unique summit, virtually bare of vegetation and open to all directions. The views over Paterson and to New York City are spectacular. Be sure to take this hike on a day when visibility is excellent.

High Mountain is located in one of the last natural areas in a heavily populated section of New Jersey. Recently, due largely to the efforts of concerned citizens, much of the mountain has been acquired by local municipalities. For years, however, the area has suffered from abuse by dirt bikes, ATVs and

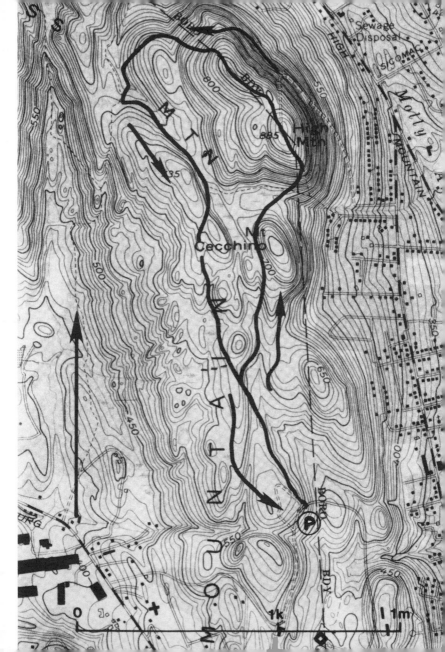

four-wheel drive vehicles. Although all motorized vehicles are now banned, ATVs may still occasionally be found on High Mountain. Bicycles are permitted, and hikers should be alert for them. The walking is made more difficult by loose rocks, torn up by motorized vehicles, and wet areas created by ruts and potholes. Garbage and graffiti are still problems, but hiking clubs are constantly working to keep the area clean. Don't be deterred; even though High Mountain is close to the metropolitan area, it is usually quiet here, and the walking is very pleasant.

Trailhead: *The hike described below starts from Parking Lot #6 at William Paterson University. If you are coming from the west, Parking Lot #6 is reached from Hamburg Turnpike (County Route 504) 1.1 miles east of Valley Road. Turn north at College Entry #5 and drive 1.1 miles along College Road to Parking Lot #6. If you are coming from the east, take Pompton Road to College Entry #1. Turn right and proceed straight ahead for one mile until you see a sign for Parking Lot #6. Turn into the parking lot, make the first left, and park on one of the uppermost tiers, near the parking lot entrance. The entire campus is normally closed for the holidays at the end of December and beginning of January. During this period, Parking Lot #6 is inaccessible (although it is possible to access the High Mountain trails from Reservoir Road in North Haledon). The campus is served by NJ Transit buses #748 from Paterson and #744 from Passaic and Paterson. Check with NJ Transit for schedules.*

Directions: From the lot, climb the embankment and cross College Road. Opposite the entrance to the parking lot, a wooden sign marks the beginning of the red-blazed trail. Bear right and begin to climb on a woods road, briefly paralleling the road below, then bear left into the woods. There are many intersecting woods roads in the area, so pay careful attention to the red blazes. After about half a mile, turn right onto a yellow-blazed trail. This trail proceeds east, soon crossing a small stream and wet area. It then curves north, passing just west of the ridge known as Mt. Cecchino. Three-quarters of a mile along the yellow trail, you will cross a small stream. From here the trail begins a steady climb to the summit of High Mountain. Halfway up, the trail bears left, bypassing a very eroded section of the road, and soon rejoins the road.

The summit of High Mountain is a thrill, even if it is abused. It is not a typical North Jersey summit of rock outcrop

The bare summit of High Mountain

framed by trees; it is more like a southern bald, grassy with a few large exposures of basaltic bedrock. To the east, one can see the immense suburban sprawl of northeastern New Jersey. On the horizon is the New York City skyline, the bridges and even a corner of the Atlantic Ocean. To the south are the Watchung ridges, to the north the Ramapos. Cross the broad summit heading northwest, following the yellow blazes on rocks, and continue downhill on the yellow trail.

After a steady descent of about 200 vertical feet on an eroded woods road, the trail levels off. Soon, you will notice a sharp left turn where the yellow blazes leave the woods road and enter the woods on a newly-cut footpath. This section of the trail is a refreshing change from the worn woods roads that you have followed up to now. Follow the yellow blazes as they gradually descend to a stream and begin to parallel the stream. Soon, the yellow trail crosses the stream and, in another 250 feet, reaches a red-blazed woods road. Turn left here and follow the red blazes southward. You will pass through an area which is often wet, but after passing a woods road which branches off to the left, the trail becomes drier.

Further down the road, you will go by several clusters of cedar trees. The red trail continues on downhill over slabs of exposed basalt and around some large puddles. After about a mile on the red trail, a white trail goes off to the right. Then, in another 500 feet, you will reach the junction with the yellow trail. Continue straight ahead on the red trail (now retracing your steps), and in another half a mile you will arrive back at Parking Lot #6, the starting point of the hike.

New Jersey Highlands Province

5

General Description: An easy-to-moderate walk, with some ups and downs, through woods and along small streams.
Type of Trail: Woods roads and graded footpaths.
Distance: 6.5 miles
Hiking Time: 4 hours
Lowest Elevation: 440 feet
Highest Elevation: 700 feet
USGS Quad: Mendham
Other Maps: NPS Jockey Hollow trail map

There are a surprising number of walking and bridle trails in the Jockey Hollow Encampment Area, one of four parcels which together constitute the Morristown National Historical Park, administered by the National Park Service. These trails (which are now maintained by the NY-NJ Trail Conference) are probably never considered by the majority of visitors who, after seeing the movie at the visitor center and visiting the quaint Wick House and the soldiers' huts, assume that they've seen all that the park has to offer. The trails in Jockey Hollow also make for excellent cross-country skiing, and the circuit described below might be used for that purpose. A four-color trail map is available at the visitor center.

Jockey Hollow is the place where Washington's army camped during the brutal winter of 1779-80. The story about the army's stay here can be found in booklets and movies at Washington's Headquarters in Morristown (which you might want to visit before or after the hike) as well as at the Jockey Hollow Visitor Center. The thing to remember while you are hiking here is that throughout these woods, brigades of soldiers from the various colonies built shelters and spent a dreadful winter. Our hike takes us past the site of Colonel John Stark's New England brigade's encampment on the easternmost face of Mt. Kemble, the Wick House, and other places of historical interest. As of this writing, visitors to Jockey Hollow are required to pay a $4.00 entrance fee at the visitor center (this fee also covers entrance to the other sections of the park — Washington's Headquarters and Fort Nonsense).

Trailhead: Take Interstate Route 287 to Exit 30B. Proceed north on U.S. Route 202 (Mt. Kemble Avenue) for 1.7 miles and turn left at the traffic light onto Tempe Wick Road. Follow Tempe Wick Road west for 1.4 miles to the park entrance, which is on the right. Pass the visitor center parking area (you may want to stop here and pick up a trail map) and follow signs to the Tour Road, a one-way loop around the park. Once on the Tour Road, bear left at the junction near the Wick House, then bear right at the soldiers' huts area, and again bear right onto Jockey Hollow Road, where there is a circular restroom building. Park at the Trail Center parking area, on the right side of the road, about 0.4 mile from this turn.

The circuit hike described below is simple, at least in concept. The six-mile-long, white-blazed Grand Loop Trail circles the park, and the Patriots' Path cuts through the middle of it. We will utilize both of these trails, together with other marked trails, to form an interesting and varied circuit. The Patriots'

Path in Jockey Hollow is not the main trunk of the Patriots' Path, which follows the valley of the Whippany River. This Patriots' Path is a footpath which starts at the New Jersey Audubon Society parking area on Hardscrabble Road, east of the New Jersey Brigade site, and connects with the main multi-use path after about six miles.

Jockey Hollow has many trails, and the plastic-covered maps posted on numbered signposts at all intersections are a great help in navigating the many trail junctions hikers will encounter. We will be referring to the numbers on these signposts throughout the hike description.

Directions: Before beginning the hike, you may wish to pick up a brochure for the self-guided Aqueduct Trail, which you will follow at the end of the hike. The brochures are available from a wooden box at the bulletin board adjacent to the parking area (they also may be obtained at the visitor center).

The hike itself begins at signpost #36 on the west side of the parking area, where you will find the Patriots' Path (metal markers, with a tree-and-river logo). Follow this trail into the woods, heading west. Almost immediately, you will cross Primrose Brook on a bridge and soon recross it on another bridge. At the **Y** junction a short distance ahead (signpost #37), bear right (still on the Patriots' Path), and soon you will emerge from the woods into the soldiers' huts area (signpost #38). (You may want to walk up the hill to the right and inspect the reconstructed huts.) Cross the road and continue on the Patriots' Path, which resumes at the rear left corner of a parking area (signpost #40). The trail now climbs uphill and soon comes to a **T** intersection (signpost #4) where you will bear right (north), following both the white-blazed Grand Loop Trail and the Patriots' Path. After a short distance, the Patriots' Path bears left into Lewis Morris Park (signpost #5). Keep right, now following only the white markers of the Grand Loop Trail, and you will immediately pass by a locked gate (signpost #6) and emerge onto a grassy clearing.

Continue straight ahead, cross the paved road (signpost #7)

and continue on the Grand Loop Trail, which now begins a steady climb of Sugar Loaf. The trail swings around the north side of the hill, passing just below the summit, then curves to the southeast and begins to descend. At the next junction (signpost #8), bear left and downhill, still following the white markers. After another quarter mile or so, the Grand Loop Trail begins to climb again, and it soon crosses paved Jockey Hollow Road (signpost #9). The trail now follows the park boundary, with houses visible to the left. Next, the trail swings to the right and proceeds downhill into deeper woods. As the trail makes a sharp left turn, a small pond may be seen below. The white-blazed trail continues to descend and soon arrives at a junction (signpost #10).

Continue straight ahead at the junction, leaving the Grand Loop Trail. You are now following a blue-blazed trail, which crosses the brook and ascends to a fork (signpost #11). Bear right here and proceed uphill, following the blue markers. Keep left at the next intersection (signpost #12) and continue uphill until you reach a locked gate (signpost #14). Here you turn right onto a gravel road, which again follows the park boundary, passing a private residence on the left. Continue along the gravel road for about 400 feet. Where the road curves to the left, follow the blue markers as they continue straight ahead at a locked gate (signpost #15) (do not follow the first road which goes off to the right). You are now on Mt. Kemble, and in another quarter of a mile you will come to Stark's brigade site (marked by a monument to the right). To the left (east), you can see the second Watchung range (note the microwave tower disguised as a tree!). The constant roar of traffic is from Interstate Route 287 in the distance. At the next intersection (signpost #16), bear right, staying with the blue trail. The trail now descends steadily. When you reach the next junction (signpost #17), make a very sharp left turn, and turn sharply right at the following junction (signpost #19), still following the blue blazes. In another quarter of a mile, just before a brook crossing, you will meet both the Patriots' Path and the Grand Loop Trail again (signpost #20). Turn left here, following the joint route of the two trails. (Proceeding straight ahead will take you back to your car.)

Follow the tree-and-river logos of the Patriots' Path and the white markers of the Grand Loop Trail south for the next mile. You will pass a junction with the Primrose Brook Trail (signpost #30) and then cross a wide wooden bridge over the brook. After crossing another brook, you will reach another junction with the Primrose Brook Trail (signpost #31) and then go over two rises. Finally, at signpost #55, turn right onto a wide, unmarked grassy road known as the Mendham Road Trail. In another quarter of a mile, cross paved Jockey Hollow Road and continue along the fence to the right, passing the visitor center on your left. When you reach the Wick House, turn right on the path leading to the house, then turn left at the entrance to the garden and pass in front of the entrance to the house (well worth a visit). This is a wonderful spot — deer are often seen grazing in the nearby field during late afternoon and early evening.

Continue straight ahead to the parking area and turn right, passing the old red barn, then follow the access road out to the main park road. Here, to the right, you will see signpost #49, which marks the beginning of the yellow-blazed Soldier Hut Trail. Proceed north on this trail, which parallels the paved road. (Make sure that you don't follow the Grand Parade Trail — also yellow-blazed — which begins at signpost #48, next to an old shack, and proceeds east, parallel to the field.) After going over a rise, the trail reaches a complex junction (signpost #50).

You have two choices here, as both routes follow the Aqueduct Trail parallel to Primrose Brook and lead back to the Trail Center parking area. (You will want to take out your brochure on this trail and read the descriptions provided for the various lettered wooden posts that you will pass along the way.) The first possibility is to turn right onto an unmarked woods road that is part of the Aqueduct Trail loop. You can follow this wide path down to signpost #34 (just before you reach paved Jockey Hollow Road), then turn left and cross the bridge over Primrose Brook. Your car is just a short walk ahead. A more interesting choice would be to bear left onto the Aqueduct Trail, marked with green blazes. (This trail has been blazed only in the clockwise direction.) It descends alongside the brook itself, crossing it six times before turning right onto the Patriots' Path at signpost #37. From this junction, the Trail Center parking area is only about a quarter of a mile away. Both of the alternative routes meet (between the fifth and sixth brook crossings of the second route) at signpost #53.

Short Hike: The yellow-blazed Soldier Hut and Grand Parade Trails can be combined to form a three-mile loop hike through the central portions of Jockey Hollow. Park at the visitor center, and walk through or around it, then go to the Wick House. Walk past the barn beyond the Wick House and pick up the yellow-blazed Soldier Hut Trail at signpost #49 (see directions above). Proceed north on this trail. After about a third of a mile, you will come to a complex junction with the unmarked Aqueduct Trail (signpost #50). Bear left here, continuing on the yellow trail. In another half a mile, at signpost #39, you will emerge onto a grassy field with some cedar trees. Continue straight ahead, cross a paved road, and climb a hill to the soldiers' huts, which are open for inspection.

After visiting the huts, return to the yellow trail and continue to climb the hill. Near the top, at signpost #41, turn right onto the Grand Parade Trail, also yellow blazed. You will now begin to descend. When you arrive at signpost #42, turn right ahead, still following the yellow blazes, and continue down to the bottom of the hill, where you will reach the Grand Parade Road at signpost #43. Bear left here and continue along the road for about 200 feet until you reach several historical markers in front of a field which commemorates the Grand Parade. Next, cross the road and reenter the woods, passing signpost #44.

In another 0.2 mile, you will reach the Trail Center parking area at signpost #45. Continue ahead, following the yellow blazes, and reenter the woods at the southern end of the parking area (signpost #35). After crossing Primrose Brook on a wooden bridge, bear left at signpost #34, then bear right, paralleling the road, and passing signpost #46. Turn right at signpost #47 and begin to parallel the field to the left. Soon you will arrive at the end of the yellow-blazed trail near an old red shack (signpost #48). Turn left, pass by the barn and the Wick House, and return to your car.

6 Pyramid Mountain Tripod Rock

General Description: A moderate hike that climbs a ridge, passing vistas and some strange and interesting boulders along the way.
Type of Trail: Rocky footpaths.
Distance: 4.7 miles
Hiking Time: 3 hours
Lowest Elevation: 640 feet
Highest Elevation: 934 feet
USGS Quad: Boonton
Other Maps: Morris County Park Commission map

Pyramid Mountain is a long ridge trending roughly north-south, with several overlooks from its summit. Its higher southern end once was the site of a fire tower, and some of the best views in the area are to be found here. Although the name "Stony Brook Mountain" has appeared for over a century on USGS topographic maps to denote the mountain just to the west, the name "Pyramid Mountain" was not used until rather recently. In the first edition (1923) of the *New York Walk Book*, hikers on the Boonton-Butler Trail were directed "to go northward between the pyramidal hill ahead and Stony Brook Mountain at the left." The mountain was first designated "Pyramid Mountain" on a topographical map published in the 1930s. In later editions of the *Walk Book*, the description of a hike along the Montville-Butler Trail includes a climb of Pyramid Mountain. In fact, the southern end of the ridge, where the fire tower once stood, does indeed resemble a pyramid when viewed from the south.

Tripod Rock, a massive boulder perched on three smaller stones, is considered by many geologists to be an extraordinary glacial erratic. Others believe it to be part of an ancient calendar site used by the Native Americans for summer solstice observations. Nearby, in the valley below, is another glacial erratic known as Bear Rock, one of the most massive single boulders in Northern New Jersey. Its relative isolation near a brook in the middle of a valley makes it an impressive sight. Pyramid Mountain also contains a unique combination of unusual geological features and some rare and endangered species of plant and animal life.

In the 1980s, developers were poised to carve the mountain ridge into building lots. Due to the efforts of the Committee to Save Pyramid Mountain, the Friends of Pyramid Mountain, and other concerned citizens, the major portion of the mountain has been acquired by the Morris County Park Commission and has been designated the Pyramid Mountain Natural Historical Area. Other lands in the area have been acquired by the State of New Jersey, the local municipalities and The Nature Conservancy, and efforts are continuing to preserve additional land in the vicinity.

Trailhead: Take Interstate 287 to Exit 44 (Main Street, Boonton). Proceed west along Main Street and turn right onto County Route 511 (Boonton Avenue). After 3.3 miles on Route 511 (about 0.8 mile north of the intersection of Route 511 and Taylortown Road, and opposite Mars Park), the Visitors Center is on the left. Park here and begin your hike from the trailhead at the parking area. It is worthwhile to stop at the Visitors Center (open on Saturday, Sunday and Monday only, and closed on holidays), which contains

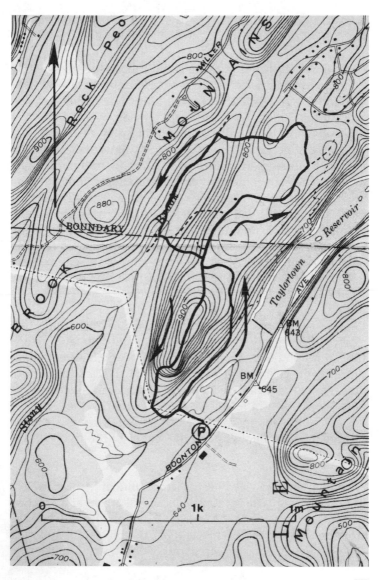

interpretive exhibits. Free hiking maps are available at the bulletin board in the parking area.

Directions: From the parking area, follow the access trail, which starts just north of a large bulletin board. In 400 feet, turn left on a dirt road. Soon, the blue-blazed Mennen Trail (part of the Butler-Montville Trail) joins from the right. Bear left, following the blue markers, and cross a stream on a wooden bridge. In another 300 feet, a yellow trail begins on your right. Turn right and follow the yellow trail north along a nearly constant contour, with huge boulders above you on the left and a camp recreation area (with a grassy ballfield, a picnic area and a small pond) below you on the right. After a quarter of a mile, an orange-blazed trail leaves to the right. Continue along the yellow trail, which soon bears left and begins to climb rather steeply. At the top of the climb, there is a viewpoint to the east. The trail now heads back into the woods and descends slightly.

Almost a mile from the start, you will reach the blue trail again. Turn right here and follow the joint blue and yellow trails through deep stands of mountain laurel. After a short distance, the yellow trail goes off to the left. Keep to the right here, and continue along the blue-blazed trail. Just past this point, look for a blue-and-white side trail on the left. This narrow trail leads in 350 feet to Lucy's Lookout, a rugged vista named for Lucy Meyer, the leader of the fight to save this mountain.

After enjoying the view, return to the blue trail and turn left. In less than a quarter of a mile, you will arrive at a junction with the white-blazed Kinnelon-Boonton Trail. Continue straight ahead (north) here, leaving the blue trail, and now following white markers. In about 500 feet, you will come to

Tripod Rock. The two matching boulders just to the north-west of Tripod Rock form a gunsight for the summer solstice sunset when viewed from a bedrock outcrop nearby. After taking some time to enjoy the site, follow the white trail north for 0.4 mile to a junction with a red-blazed trail which leaves to the left.

At the junction, proceed straight ahead, continuing to follow the white blazes. In about 650 feet, you will notice an orange-blazed trail which leaves to the right. Turn right and follow this trail (the northern end of the orange trail which you first passed earlier on the hike) for 75 feet to a rocky vista known as Ken's Lookout. This spot is named for Ken Lloyd, a dedicated trail maintainer who helped in the fight to preserve this beautiful area. After taking in the view, retrace your steps back to the white trail, turn left, and follow the white trail back to the junction with the red trail.

Tripod Rock

Now turn right onto the red trail, which goes through interesting, remote and rugged mountain scenery. In about a third of a mile, you will see a house directly ahead. Here the trail turns sharply left and climbs to the top of Eagle Cliff. The trail once followed the edge of this cliff, but it has been relocated to a safer route further west. After passing a huge balanced rock to the left – a glacial erratic known as Whale Head Rock — the trail bears left and begins a steep descent.

At the base of the descent, the trail crosses a branch of Bear House Brook and then the brook itself and reaches a junction with the blue trail. Turn left here, and in another half mile you will come to the awesome Bear Rock (also known as "Bare Roke") — a gigantic glacial erratic sitting at the edge of a swamp. This rock was probably used as a shelter in precolonial times by Native Americans. From Bear Rock, turn left and follow the blue and white trails across Bear House Brook on a plank bridge. Just ahead, turn right onto the yellow trail again. In a third of a mile, this trail will bring you up to the ridge, through a dense stand of laurel. Now turn right onto the blue trail and follow it as it gradually climbs to the highest elevation on the Pyramid Mountain ridge, where you will find several overlooks on exposed slabs of rock. The New York City skyline is visible to the east. Continuing on the blue trail, you descend steeply to the power line cut and high-voltage towers, passing a red-blazed trail, which begins to the right near the bottom of the hill. At the high-voltage tower, the white trail leaves to the right. Turn left here, continuing along the blue trail, and descend stone steps. Soon after joining a dirt road coming in from the right, you will cross the stream on a wooden bridge, then bear right, leaving the blue trail, and follow the Visitors Center access trail back to your car.

7 Ramapo Mountain State Forest

General Description: A moderate hike involving a climb to a lake and then up to a ridge that offers some excellent vistas.
Type of Trail: Rocky footpaths.
Distance: 3.5 miles
Hiking Time: 2 hours
Lowest Elevation: 400 feet
Highest Elevation: 740 feet
USGS Quad: Wanaque
Other Maps: NYNJTC North Jersey Trails — Map #22, NJ Walk Book Map #20, DEP map

Sitting high above Oakland and the Ramapo River is beautiful Ramapo Lake. Like any other reasonably accessible body of water in New Jersey (it is an easy walk from Skyline Drive), it draws a crowd on weekends. The parking area may be quite full, but the vast majority of the people will be going no further than the lake. Our hike will take us to the hills surrounding the lake, which offer good views and are excellent examples of glaciated Highland topography. It will include a few steep climbs, several expansive views, and some deep woods walking.

Trailhead: Take Interstate Route 287 to Exit 57 (Skyline Drive), and proceed north on Skyline Drive. Just ahead on the left is the Ramapo Mountain State Forest parking area.

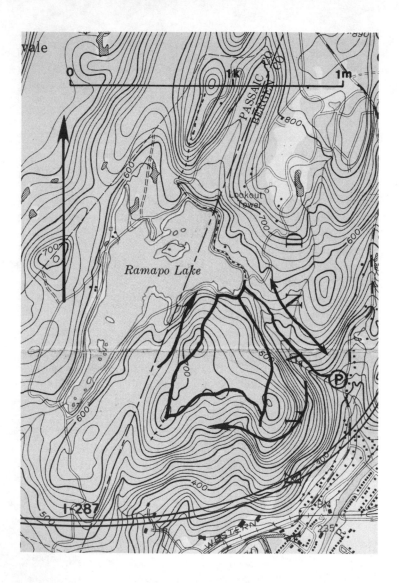

Directions: From the parking area, follow the blue-blazed MacEvoy Trail, which leads uphill to the lake. For much of the way, it follows a brook with several cascades (most attractive in the spring or after a heavy rain). At the lake, turn left and cross the concrete roadway/spillway, then — in another 100 feet — turn left again, back into the woods, on the red-blazed Lookout Trail. After rising briefly, the red trail dips down to parallel a stream (the other side of the stream that we followed on the way up to the lake), then begins a steady climb for about a quarter of a mile. The trail then levels off, passes a large rock ledge to the left, and begins to descend slightly, soon reaching a fork in the trail. The red blazes turn right, but we will continue straight ahead on an unmarked trail that leads in 350 feet to a good viewpoint over Oakland and beyond to High Mountain. On a clear day, the New York City skyline can be seen in the distance. I-287 is visible to the left (unfortunately, the sounds of the traffic are quite audible, even at this distance). After enjoying this rocky vista, backtrack to the fork in the Lookout Trail and bear left, now once again following the red markers.

The red trail continues at about the same elevation, with several short but steep ups and downs, for about two-thirds of a mile. Here, after a short climb, you will reach a junction with the yellow-blazed Hoeferlin Trail. A few steps ahead along this trail is a viewpoint to the west through some pine trees. The Wyanokies stand out in sharp contrast against the horizon. Return to the junction and turn left on the joint Hoeferlin/Lookout Trail, with both yellow and red blazes. You will soon reach a rock ledge with a limited view over Ramapo Lake. Then, after crossing a seasonal stream, the trail climbs to a rock outcrop with an expansive view of Ramapo Lake below. From here, the trail descends steadily and soon ends at the shore of the lake. The beginning of the

Lookout Trail (where you started up the mountain) is a short distance to your right, and just beyond is the blue-blazed MacEvoy Trail which you took to the lake. Cross the dam, turn right into the woods on the blue trail and descend to your car.

Longer Hike: If you have more time and energy, you may wish to hike along the northern shore of the lake and then climb to the ruins of a burned-out mansion that resembles a castle. From the dam at the junction with the MacEvoy Trail, follow the roadway along the north shore of the lake. After passing a residence, turn right on a gravel road that swings off to the right and heads uphill. Where the road turns right, turn left onto the white-blazed Castle Point Trail, which leads steeply uphill to the castle ruins and some excellent views. Continue along the trail to find other ruins and vistas, then retrace your steps to the dam.

Ramapo Lake

8 Ringwood State Park

General Description: A moderate hike that begins at an historical site, passes a lake (swimming possibilities), climbs a mountain and passes by botanical gardens.
Type of Trail: Rocky footpaths, woods roads and service lanes.
Distance: 5.5 miles
Hiking Time: 3-4 hours
Lowest Elevation: 400 feet
Highest Elevation: 1,040 feet
USGS Quad: Greenwood Lake, Ramsey, Sloatsburg
Other Maps: NYNJTC North Jersey Trails — Map #22, NJ Walk Book Map #20, DEP map

There is much history at Ringwood Manor, and it begins in 1740 with the formation of the Ringwood Company. This was the site of important iron-making activities which aided Washington and his army during the Revolutionary War. The manor house has a complex history of its own and is well stocked with pieces of period furniture. While you are here, you may wish to tour the house and grounds and learn more about its history from the guides. Also in this state park is Skylands Manor, with its beautiful botanical gardens. Our hike will take us through this area and to Shepherd Lake, which offers swimming and boating.

In recent years, *Ringwood State Park* has become very popular with mountain bike riders, who have been welcomed by

the park management. Recently, signs have been posted with international symbols on brown plastic wands, indicating the permitted uses of each segment of every trail. Since several portions of this hike include trails that are open to mountain bikes, hikers should be alert to their presence.

Trailhead: *Take Interstate Route 287 to Exit 57 (Skyline Drive). Proceed north on Skyline Drive, and follow it to its end at County Route 511 (Greenwood Lake Turnpike). Turn right, follow Route 511 north for 1.5 miles, and then turn right onto Sloatsburg Road. (There is a sign for Ringwood State Park here.) Continue on Sloatsburg Road for 2.4 miles. When you see a sign indicating the entrance to Ringwood State Park, bear left and enter the park (a $3 fee may be charged during summer months). There is a pond on the left, and the manor house is facing you. Continue past the first two large parking areas. After the second parking area, turn left and park opposite a refreshment stand on the left side of the road. To the right, two wooden bridges cross the brook. This is the trailhead.*

Directions: The overall plan is to follow the red-blazed Ringwood-Ramapo Trail to the green-dot Halifax Trail, and continue on this green trail to the white-blazed Crossover Trail. You will notice signposts for red, white and yellow trails at the trailhead by the bridges. Follow the red trail across the bridges, and you will soon reach Sloatsburg Road. After crossing the road, the white-blazed Crossover Trail comes in from the right (this will eventually be your return route).

The red trail bears left and climbs rather steeply up Cupsaw Mountain. At the top of the rise, the yellow trail comes in from the right and joins the red trail for about 200 feet. Continue on the red trail, which soon bears right as the yellow trail goes off to the left. Almost immediately, you will come upon a trail shelter (built by The Hiking, Eating, Arguing and Puzzle Solving Club of the Cooper Union), after which the trail begins to descend. It then turns left on a woods road, the route of the blue-blazed Cupsaw Brook Trail. After a short distance, the blue trail leaves, going off to the left. Then, in another 50 feet, the red trail leaves to the left. Continue along the red trail, which soon crosses the brook and begins to parallel it on the other side. There are some wet areas here, and you may have to look carefully in places to find the trail route. After a while, the trail begins to climb and, about half a mile from the brook crossing, it turns left on an old road and soon reaches a paved road at a traffic circle near Shepherd Lake.

Turn right on the paved road, then immediately left, following the sign in the middle of the traffic circle for the boat launch. Continue straight ahead on a road along the lake shore (do not turn right and go up the hill towards the stone chapel), soon passing the boathouse and re-entering the woods. Continue following the red trail along the woods road (don't turn right onto an unmarked trail which parallels the road for a short distance and then goes off into the woods). After 0.3 mile, follow the red trail as it turns off the road and begins to head uphill. The trail crosses another road and, after climbing more steeply, reaches the top of a hill. It descends a bit, crosses a bike trail, passes an old foundation, crosses the right-of-way of a buried gas line, and climbs Mt. Defiance. Just below the 1,040-foot summit, there is a good viewpoint to the west and north over the Sterling Ridge.

From the summit you begin a rather steep descent, still following the red blazes. Soon you will pass some impressive cliffs to the right and reach an intersection with the green-dot Halifax Trail. (There is a good vista from a rocky knoll to the right of the red trail about 500 feet beyond this intersection.) To continue with the circuit, turn right onto the green trail and you will soon begin to descend on a series of gradual switchbacks — the remnants of an old carriage road. Near the top of this descent, a short unmarked trail on the right leads uphill to a vista overlooking Skylands Manor.

At the base of the descent, the green trail ends at a gravel road with white blazes. This is the Crossover Trail, which links Ringwood Manor with the Ramapos. Turn right and continue along the white-blazed road for 0.2 mile, passing two roads which go off to the left. Soon you will see a paved road ahead. Turn right on this road and walk by the gardens of Skylands Manor. You may wish to stop off at the manor house and take a tour. Film crews and wedding parties often use this beautiful area.

Continue following the white blazes along this paved tourist road. You will walk by a lodge with a sundial clock on its chimney and then pass a parking area to the right, with a map of the area on a large bulletin board. Bear left at a fork, and you will soon go between two concrete eagles (which mark the entrance to the Skylands Manor area). Just after crossing the intersecting road, the white trail bears left and re-enters the woods. If you prefer, you may continue straight ahead downhill on the paved road for 0.4 mile to rejoin the white trail. (See map.)

Having left civilization, the trail heads downhill and follows paths and woods roads through overgrown farmland, crossing some very wet areas. In about half a mile, you will make a right turn onto the route of a gas pipeline and go along the left side of a fenced-in area. Soon the trail turns left onto the paved road (Morris Avenue) and, in another 450 feet, crosses a bridge over Cupsaw Brook. The trail continues along the road for another 100 feet and then turns right, re-entering the woods. After a gentle climb, the white trail turns left and briefly joins the yellow trail. At a **T** intersection, the white trail goes off to the right on a woods road, while the yellow trail turns left. Continue on the white trail for another half mile, and you will meet the red trail which you started on. Turn left, cross Sloatsburg Road and the two bridges over the stream, and you'll be back at the trailhead.

9 The Wyanokie Plateau

General Description: A moderate-to-strenuous hike leading to old iron mines, up rocky summits with excellent views, through woods and along streams.

Type of Trail: Woods roads and rocky footpaths, with some use of hands required.

Distance: 7.5 miles

Hiking Time: 5 hours

Lowest Elevation: 400 feet

Highest Elevation: 1,100 feet

USGS Quad: Wanaque

Other Maps: NYNJTC North Jersey Trails — Map #21, NJ Walk Book Map #21, Weis Ecology Center map

The 34-square-mile area of the Wyanokie Highlands, which includes the 3,907-acre Norvin Green State Forest, has one of most extensive trail networks in the state of New Jersey. Most of these trails were originally blazed by Montclair College professor Will S. Monroe and the Green Mountain Club in the 1920s. The trails climb up and down the several peaks that collectively form what is known as the Wyanokie Plateau. Some trails lead to high points with spectacular views. The climbs can be quite steep and traverse rocky terrain, making this area a challenging place to hike.

Most of the mountain summits are partly bare, except for

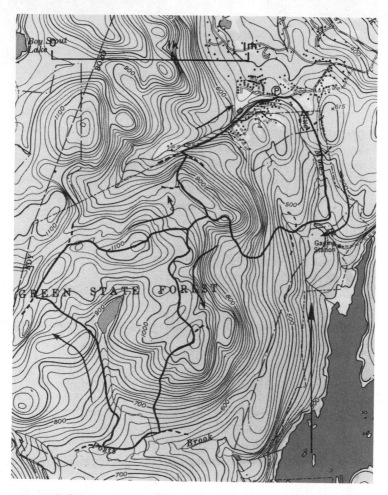

some pitch pine and scrub oak, and they offer some excellent views. Although it is not the highest point in the area, Wyanokie High Point gives one the impression that it is, commanding views to the north out to New York state and to the east, over the Ramapos and Watchungs, to New York City. Here and elsewhere on the plateau there is much evidence of former glacial activity, with numerous glacial erratics dotting the summits and high bare areas. Glacial chattermarks and striations are also evident. In addition, the summit rock outcroppings exhibit exfoliation, a process in which the decomposing and weathering bedrock breaks apart in large flakes.

In recent years, gypsy moths have devastated the oak forests that dominate the Wyanokie Plateau, and this significant environmental change will be in evidence throughout the course of this hike. Thousands of trees have been defoliated, and most are either dead or dying. During summer months, hikers will find themselves exposed to the sun far more than one would normally expect in heavily forested New Jersey, and some hikers may wish to take precautions. Increased sunlight reaching the forest floor has resulted in the explosive growth of grasses, which often obscure the trail, and of blueberries (which ripen in early July).

The trails in this area are numerous and multicolored. Often the trail colors (red, green, blue, etc.) are painted over a white background to improve visibility. In many sections, you will notice that two trails share the same route for a distance. Pay close attention to avoid missing the turnoffs you want to take. In many of the summit areas where bare rock predominates, trails are marked with paint blazes on the bedrock itself. In some cases, these can be faint, so look closely. On these exposed bedrock areas, turns are often designated by a paint mark curving in the direction of the turn.

Although the central portion of this beautiful area is protected state land, much of the land to the north is privately owned. In recent years, a private landowner closed his land to public access. The hike described in the previous editions of this book traversed this property. Due to the closure of the trails on this land, the hike has been revised to include trails that remain open to the public. It leads to rocky summits with outstanding views and explores some wild and less-visited areas of Norvin Green State Forest. While the hike described below is challenging and offers a good workout, there is an excellent option for a shorter hike, or bail-out, which will be noted in the text.

Trailhead: From County Route 511 (Ringwood Avenue) in Wanaque, proceed west on West Brook Road and cross over the Wanaque Reservoir. After traveling 1.5 miles on West Brook Road, you will reach a Y intersection with Stonetown Road. Bear left, staying on West Brook Road, and in another half a mile, turn left onto Snake Den Road. Follow this road uphill, keeping to the left at the intersection with Dale Road. In 0.6 mile, you will reach a large parking area on the right side of the road, just before the entrance to the Weis Ecology Center. Park here.

Before beginning the hike, you may wish to stop at the visitor center. From the parking area, enter the Weis Ecology Center grounds on a dirt road. Bear right and follow the road to the red-brick visitor center, which is open Wednesday through Sunday, 8:30 a.m. to 4:30 p.m. Free trail maps are available at the visitor center. If the building is closed, trail maps and other information may be available at a kiosk in front of the building.

Directions: From the parking area, turn left and walk back along Snake Den Road for about 150 feet. When the green blazes end, turn right and follow the red-dot-on-white blazes of the Wyanokie Circular Trail and the yellow-dot-on-white blazes of the Mine Trail, passing alongside the backyards of private residences. In 0.2 mile, the yellow blazes go off to the right. Continue straight ahead, following the red blazes. The yellow trail will cross the red trail in another 600 feet; continue ahead on the red trail. About 400 feet beyond this point, you will notice an unmarked trail going off to the left. (As of this writing, it is planned to blaze this trail orange.) Turn left onto this trail (which is actually an old mining road) and follow it for about 600 feet to the entrance to the Roomy Mine.

This iron mine, which was first opened in 1840 and has been abandoned since 1890, features a passage which extends into the hillside for about 100 feet. To enter the mine, you will first have to crawl through a narrow opening, but once you're inside, the mine is high enough to stand upright. If you're planning to explore the mine, a good flashlight is essential, and a hard hat is also advisable. The floor of the mine may be wet, but if you're properly prepared, the horizontal shaft — drilled deep into the bedrock — is a fascinating highlight of the hike.

Once you've explored the mine, continue ahead on the trail, which is now marked with yellow dot blazes. After a short distance, you will reach the red trail and turn left, now following the joint yellow and red trails.

In another quarter of a mile, the trail turns right to cross a stream on a footbridge. Before proceeding across the stream, continue ahead for 100 feet. To the left, you will notice a large water-filled shaft. This is the Blue Mine, another iron mine, which was worked extensively during the nineteenth century. A large concrete pad, which was once used to anchor heavy machinery, is located immediately in front of the mine.

After visiting this mine, cross the stream and continue ahead on the marked trail, soon passing the remains of an old shelter to the right. Continue ahead on the red trail when the yellow trail leaves to the right. After passing the northern end of the white-blazed Lower Trail, you will begin a steady climb. This rather strenuous climb — the longest on the hike — leads to the rocky Wyanokie High Point, with its spectacular 360^0 view. You'll look down over the Wanaque Reservoir, with the Manhattan skyline visible in the distance.

Once you have savored the views from this idyllic spot, scramble down the rocky face, following the red dots painted on the rocks. In 250 feet, at the base of the steep descent, you will reach a junction with the blue-blazed Hewitt-Butler Trail (which is also the route of the Highlands Trail, with teal diamond blazes). Turn left, now following the joint route of all three trails. (If you elect to shorten your hike due to time constraints, or if you have found it challenging enough and wish to avoid the long stretch ahead of you, turn right here and jump to the last paragraph of the hike description.) When the red trail leaves to the right in another 0.2 mile, continue straight ahead, following the blue and teal diamond blazes.

Soon afterwards, you will reach a rock outcrop from which, looking back along the trail, Wyanokie High Point is visible. This spot is known as Yoo-Hoo Point, since it provides the opportunity for hikers to call back to their friends at the High Point. In recent years, this vista has become overgrown in places, and you may have to look around a little to find it. The trail continues along the ridge and, in another half a mile — after a short, steep climb — it reaches the summit of Carris Hill, where the yellow-blazed Carris Hill Trail begins to the left. (A short walk along the Carris Hill Trail leads to an expansive view over the Wanaque Reservoir.) Continue ahead on the blue trail which, after traversing another rocky high point, begins a steady descent. Be sure to follow the blue blazes, and do not turn off onto any unmarked woods roads or tracks.

You've reached the halfway point of the hike when the blue trail turns right on a woods road, and the white-blazed Post Brook Trail begins to the left. Turn right, still following the blue trail, which immediately crosses a stream. Hikers may wish to follow this stream down to Post Brook, just a short distance away. This stream confluence offers more in the way of water than will be found elsewhere on this hike, and on hot days it may be refreshing to tired feet. Continue heading west along the blue trail and, in another 0.3 mile, make a very sharp right turn onto the yellow-blazed Wyanokie Crest Trail.

You are now entering one of the wildest areas of Norvin Green State Forest. After a quarter of a mile, the trail turns sharply left and begins to follow a tributary of Post Brook, twice crossing the stream on rocks. The footing — over large boulders — is often quite rough, but this section of the hike is very scenic, particularly when the water level is high. Hikers should be alert for poison ivy, which grows among the boulders in some of the upstream sections. After following the stream for half a mile, the trail bears left and soon begins a rather steep ascent. It passes some interesting erratic boulders and continues to ascend more gradually.

When you reach the highest point, you will find an orange-blazed trail going off to the right. The blazes may be a little faint, so you should look carefully for this junction. Turn right and follow this orange trail, which leads in a quarter of a mile to the red-on-white-blazed Wyanokie Circular Trail, passing a small vernal pond on the way. When you reach the red trail, turn right and proceed through a very dense mountain laurel thicket. After crossing an old woods road, you will traverse two rocky outcroppings.

In about a mile from the end of the orange-blazed trail, you'll come to a junction with the blue-blazed Hewitt-Butler Trail. This spot should be familiar, as you were here earlier in the hike. Continue ahead on the joint red-and-blue trail, retracing your steps for 0.2 mile. The last part of this section is steeply uphill. When the red trail leaves to the right, bear left, following the blue blazes. The blue trail continues along the ridge, passing several viewpoints to the left.

Soon after the white-blazed Macopin Trail departs to the left, you will reach the last viewpoint and begin a steady descent. The trail is now rather steep, and you will want to proceed cautiously, especially if the tread is wet or icy. In about a third of a mile, the yellow-on-white-blazed Mine Trail comes in from the right. Turn left, now following both yellow and blue blazes, and soon reach a wide woods road — the route of the green-blazed Otter Hole Trail. Turn right, and continue along the road, which becomes paved after 500 feet. Bear left at a **Y** intersection, and you will soon reach the parking area of the Weis Ecology Center, where your car is parked.

10 The Torne

General Description: An easy-to-moderate hike that climbs over boulders and bare rock to excellent vistas, and finishes with a steep descent.
Type of Trail: Rocky footpaths; use of hands required in places.
Distance: 1.7 miles
Hiking Time: 1.5 hours
Lowest Elevation: 860 feet
Highest Elevation: 1,120 feet
USGS Quad: Wanaque
Other Maps: NYNJTC North Jersey Trails — Map #21, NJ Walk Book Map #20

In the southern portion of Norvin Green State Forest is the *Torne*, which offers the hiker exceptional views over mostly undeveloped land to the south and west. For nearly half a mile along its south-facing summit slopes, the Hewitt-Butler Trail traverses a series of glacially polished rock outcrops, each one with a slightly different angle of view over the near and distant mountain scenery. For a small effort, the Torne repays the hiker with some of the best views in the Wyanokies.

Trailhead: Take Interstate Route 287 to Exit 53 (Bloomingdale) and turn left onto Hamburg Turnpike. Upon entering

Bloomingdale, the name of the road changes to Main Street. After 1.4 miles (from Route 287), you will reach a fork in the road. Bear right, and in another 0.1 mile turn right (uphill) onto Glenwild Avenue. Continue ahead for 3.2 miles, and park in a parking area to the right, near the trailhead to Otter Hole.

Directions: At the eastern end of the parking area, cross Glenwild Avenue. You will note a blue-blazed post, marked "HB." Follow this blue-blazed Hewitt-Butler Trail, which climbs the hill and then turns right, heading west and parallel to the road, for about 0.25 mile. Here, with the road visible to the right, you will come to an intersection with the

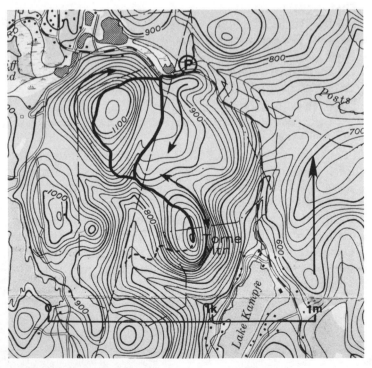

red-blazed Torne Trail. Turn left on this red trail, proceeding south and then down along the side of a gully, which soon becomes very rocky and boulder-filled. In about 0.5 mile, the red trail ends at a second junction with the blue trail, which crosses the gully amidst large boulders.

(Option: From this junction, you may wish to turn left and follow the blue markers for about 0.35 mile, most of it uphill, to several viewpoints. The large glacial erratics on the right after 0.2 mile offer good views of the bare rock slopes of the Torne to the west. Farther along the trail, you'll reach the graffiti-scarred summit of this hill, with excellent views to the east, including the Wanaque Reservoir and, on a clear day, the New York City skyline. High Mountain near Paterson and the unsightly scar of I-287 are also visible. Although the topographic map labels this summit and overlook as the Torne, hikers generally call it South Torne or Osio Rock, the latter of which appears on the Trail Conference map. If you choose this option, you need to retrace your steps to the junction of the red and blue trails.)

From the junction of the red and blue trails in the gully, turn right and head west and uphill, following the blue markers. (If you've taken the side trip to Osio Rock, you should just continue straight ahead at the junction.) For the next half mile, as you gradually climb the Torne (North Torne), there are a series of bedrock outcrops that offer constantly changing views to the south. Many large rounded boulders in the vicinity reveal the extensive glaciation this area once experienced. With a snow cover, this section may be difficult to follow, as most of the markers are on the bedrock itself.

Near what seems to be the highest point of the mountain, at a westerly viewpoint (the next to last on the hike), are a number of man-made rock slab chairs (nine chairs and a love-seat) in a semi-circle. These modern megaliths are found just to the right (southeast) of the trail, and their exact location is not easy to describe. From this vicinity, the trail swings through a wooded section to the final viewpoint, this one looking to the north and west. From here, the blue trail descends the mountain rather steeply and, in about a quarter mile, it reaches the first junction with the red trail. Continue on the blue trail back to the parking area.

11

Bearfort Mountain

General Description: A long but moderate hike through deep woods to a pond and along rocky ridges, some with vistas.
Type of Trail: Woods roads and rocky footpaths.
Distance: 6 miles
Hiking Time: 4 hours
Lowest Elevation: 700 feet
Highest Elevation: 1,300 feet
USGS Quad: Greenwood Lake
Other Maps: NYNJTC North Jersey Trails — Map #21, NJ Walk Book Map #19

With its many overlooks, colorful bedrock and stunted pitch pines, *Bearfort Mountain* is one of the most picturesque mountain ridges in all of New Jersey. Here, hikers can find several small lakes or ponds and miles of marked trail. While the Bearfort ridge attains a maximum elevation of about 1,450 feet near Terrace Pond, the vertical rise from Pinecliff Lake (just a mile to the east and at an elevation of about 640 feet) makes it comparable to the relief of the Kittatinny ridge. The comparison with the Kittatinny ridge is also appropriate on a geological basis, since both are tilted sedimentary ridges that have become mountainous due to differential erosion. Bearfort Mountain is unique in that it occurs in the midst of the Highlands Province and yet is substantially different in origin. Geologists believe that it was once a sound in an ancient sea into which were poured sediments washed from surrounding mountains.

Trailhead: Take N.J. Route 23 to Newfoundland, and proceed north on Union Valley Road (County Route 513) to West Milford. Bear left at the shopping center. After passing Camp Hope, keep to the right at the fork and continue to Warwick Turnpike, which is about half a mile ahead. Turn left on Warwick Turnpike, follow it a short distance uphill, and park on the right-hand side of the road just past a concrete bridge (and before reaching White Road). There are other pull-outs farther west on Warwick Turnpike if additional space is needed for parking. The trailhead for the Bearfort Ridge Trail is on the eastern side of this bridge.

Directions: Follow the white-blazed Bearfort Ridge Trail uphill through hemlocks to the spot where it turns left onto a woods road. Although the white markings will soon veer off to the left on a footpath, stay on the woods road, known as the Quail Trail, which is marked with orange blazes. This road passes through some very beautiful hemlock growth, and gradually climbs to the Bearfort Ridge. En route, three streams are crossed, the last of which is Cooley Brook, the outlet stream of Surprise Lake. The road becomes less distinct around the second stream crossing, but after a while, it becomes more obvious (although in places, the trail has been routed off the road to bypass some wet areas). After two and one-half miles, the orange trail ends at a junction with the yellow Ernest Walter Trail, very close to Surprise Lake. Bear right, following the yellow trail, and almost immediately you will reach a clearing, with the lake visible to the left.

From here, you might consider taking a short side trip to one of New Jersey's best overlooks. To do so, continue north on the yellow trail, soon crossing a wet area, and then ascend to the ridge. Here, among the pitch pines, there is a viewpoint over Greenwood Lake to the east. Continue north along the trail for another 0.2 mile until you come to a well-elevated, glacially polished rock outcrop which offers unobstructed views out over Greenwood Lake and to the Wyanokies, with New York City visible in the distance. After enjoying the views, retrace your steps and return to Surprise Lake.

(It should be pointed out that in recent years, a mysterious painter-outer blacked out many of the blazes on both the yellow and white trails in this area. Trail Conference maintainers repeatedly reblazed the trails, but the mystery person often returned to cover up his work. It seems that this vandal has not been around much lately, but if you find that the markings in this section have been blacked out, just follow the black blazes.)

From Surprise Lake, continue south on the yellow trail, passing through thick rhododendron. After a stream crossing and a short climb, you will come to a junction with the white-blazed Bearfort Ridge Trail. Follow the white markings south along one of the main ridges, through pitch pine and over conglomerate "puddingstone" rock — quite unusual for this area. In about a third of a mile, after climbing a little, you'll reach a viewpoint. Then, in about another half a mile — after some minor ups and downs — you'll come to one of the most interesting features of the hike. A large section of rock has split away from the main rock formation, creating a deep crevice just to the right of the trail, which overlooks an attractive swamp. This is a nice spot to sit down and rest for a little while.

In another mile, after traversing some very long rock out-

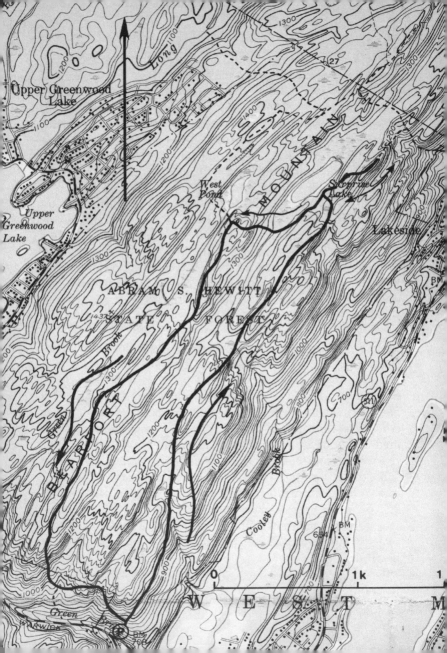

crops and descending slightly, you'll come to a final viewpoint out to the south and west. This viewpoint is off the trail to the right. From this vantage point, a cross-section of the Bearfort Mountain ridge can be seen in the gap utilized by the Warwick Turnpike. The gap is quite deep and has exposed the layering and extreme tilting of the sedimentary deposits that make up the mountain. From here it is about a mile downhill, descending sometimes quite steeply, to the woods road (turn right) and the parking area.

Longer Hike: It is possible to take a longer hike by adding another loop. Although the length of the hike is increased by only 1.7 miles, the added loop has some strenuous ups-and-downs. If you wish to take this longer route, follow the yellow trail north from Surprise Lake to the overlook described above. Continue north for another 700 feet, descending steadily to a junction with the blue-on-white State Line Trail, and bear left. The State Line Trail gradually ascends (with some minor dips along the way) until, in about half a mile, it reaches the Appalachian Trail (A.T.) on the ridgetop. At this point, you might wish to take a side trip north on the A.T. into New York State to a lookout known as Grand View, an unusually open area with excellent views. It's about half a mile north on the A.T., and you'll know it when you get there. Retrace your steps back to the junction of the State Line Trail and the A.T., and head southwest on the A.T. In about 0.3 mile — after passing a limited viewpoint to the east, and then descending very steeply — you will meet the yellow-blazed Ernest Walter Trail again. Turn left and follow it for about a mile, past West Pond, to its junction with the white-blazed Bearfort Ridge Trail. At first, the going along this trail is quite easy, but after two-thirds of a mile, the going becomes much rougher, with some very steep descents and ascents. After crossing the outlet stream of West Pond, the trail ascends steeply to a junction with a side trail that leads left for about 100 feet to a nice viewpoint over the pond. About 0.1 mile beyond this junction, you will reach the white trail. Turn right here, and follow that trail for about three miles, back to your car, using the description provided above.

Bearfort Ridge

12 Terrace Pond

General Description: A long but not too strenuous hike that winds among the various ridges of Bearfort Mountain and passes near a gem of a mountain pond.

Type of Trail: Very rocky footpaths, with some use of hands required, and woods roads.

Distance: 4.8 miles

Hiking Time: 3.5 hours

Lowest Elevation: 1,100 feet

Highest Elevation: 1,450 feet

USGS Quad: Wawayanda

Other Maps: NYNJTC North Jersey Trails — Map #21, NJ Walk Book Map #19, NWCDC map

Terrace Pond, a natural mountain lake, is located on the wide summit ridge of Bearfort Mountain south of Warwick Turnpike. It is within the Bearfort Mountain Natural Area of Wawayanda State Park. In the years since I first visited Terrace Pond, it has changed from a privately-owned but isolated place of great beauty, to a heavily littered hangout for beer hikers, to a beautiful place with graffiti scars and rules and regulations. What really opened up Terrace Pond to the general public was not public ownership but a gas line; its installation required a massive cut over the mountain. Previously, one had to walk over rocky footpaths for nearly two miles before coming to this wonder of the Bearfort ridge. Now you can walk easily, albeit uphill, for much of the way along a path nearly 100 feet wide.

Nonetheless, Terrace Pond is well worth a visit, and this hike is one of the best in this book. The place has a special magic, with its steep cliffs plunging down to deep blue water. Scrub pines jut out along purple conglomerate walls, making the setting appear almost prehistoric. On this hike you will encounter striking overlooks, and you will walk on both cut trail and woods roads. The first part of the hike is relatively easy, but the last part involves some steep descents and climbs where you will have to use your hands as well as your feet. This Terrace Pond hike is central Bearfort Mountain at its best.

Trailhead: *The Bearfort Waters parking area is on the west side of Clinton Road about 1.7 miles south of Warwick Turnpike, at the southern end of Upper Greenwood Lake. From N.J. Route 23, go north on Union Valley Road (County Route 513), head west on Warwick Turnpike, and turn left on Clinton Road, the first major left as you pass Upper Greenwood Lake on your right. (You can also follow Clinton Road for 7.3 miles north from N.J. Route 23, which is a more direct route.) If you come from the north, the parking area, which has been designated by the Newark Watershed as Parking Area #7 (although no posted signs indicate the number) is about a quarter mile south of the gas line cut. If you come from the south, the parking area is just north of the entrance to the Wildcat Mountain Wilderness site (Project U.S.E.).*

Directions: From the parking area, cross the road and enter the woods on a cut trail marked with yellow and blue blazes. Almost immediately, the yellow-blazed Terrace Pond South Trail turns right. Follow this yellow trail. (The blue-blazed Terrace Pond North Trail, which goes off to the left, will be your return route.) You will soon find yourself in deep woods, walking through a large stand of mountain laurel and white pines, and crossing several swampy areas on

plank puncheons. In about 0.6 mile, the trail goes through a magnificent rhododendron grove, with the large rhododendrons forming an arch over the trail in places. After running along an interesting whaleback rock and crossing a low stone wall, you will reach a woods road. Turn left onto the road, and then left again onto another road, continuing to follow the yellow markers. In another half a mile, the yellow markers bear very sharply left at a junction of woods roads. Continue along the yellow trail, which turns left at the top of a rise, with another woods road going off to the right here. About half a mile beyond the sharp left turn, the trail bears right, bypassing a flooded section of the road, and crosses the outlet of a swamp on rocks. In wet seasons, there is an attractive cascade to the right of the trail. The trail goes over two concrete pipes, and just beyond, you will come to a fork.

Here you will bear right and follow the yellow-on-white markers of the Yellow Dot Trail, a pleasant woods road. In a quarter of a mile, the red-on-white blazed Terrace Pond Red Trail comes in from the left. In another 100 feet, you will reach a fork in the road. Here, the red trail turns right, while the Yellow Dot Trail goes left. Bear left, continuing on the Yellow Dot Trail. In another 0.6 mile, the woods road ends, and the yellow-on-white markers head uphill on a rather steep footpath. Where the trail levels off on a rock outcrop, you will find an excellent viewpoint to the east, on the left and off the trail. A number of glacial erratics are here, one of which is perched on smaller stones. Note that you are on a ridge that is west of the easternmost of the several ridges on Bearfort Mountain. On a clear day, the New York City skyline is visible.

From this viewpoint, return to the trail, which will soon again ascend steeply and then end at a white-blazed trail on top of a long rock outcrop, with some pitch pines. Bear right, and follow these white blazes along the rock outcrop, through the woods, past an enormous propped boulder, and finally out to a rock ledge, with a view over the pond. From here, the trail descends very steeply and soon reaches a **T** junction. The white markers go to the right, but you will want to make a slight detour on the path to the left, which leads to another rock outcrop directly overlooking the pond.

Terrace Pond

After enjoying the view, continue north on the white trail, paralleling the edge of the cliffs.

Where the blue-blazed Terrace Pond North Trail (coming in from the right) meets this white trail, bear left and down to the outlet of the pond, following both white and blue blazes. This descent is very steep, and you will have to use your hands in places. After crossing the outlet on a plank bridge, the trail begins to ascend. Soon, an unmarked trail to the left leads to another nice viewpoint over the pond. After enjoying the view of water and cliffs, continue along the trail for a short distance to another junction. Here, the white trail leaves to the left. Continue straight ahead, following the blue-blazed Terrace Pond North Trail. After crossing several wet areas on planks and rotted logs, you will come to a rocky area, with a rounded outcrop — offering good views to the west — just to the left of the trail. Continue on the blue trail, soon passing by an underground stream to the right of the trail. After several short, steep descents, you will finally come out onto the gas line cut. Bear left here and continue for about 450 feet to the bottom of the hill. Here, the blue trail re-enters the woods on your left and leads in about half a mile — over relatively level terrain — to the trailhead and your car. Another alternative, sensible in wet weather, is to take the gas line cut to the road, turn left, and walk back to your car along the pavement.

13 Pequannock Watershed Bearfort Fire Tower

General Description: A moderate hike through forest along the Bearfort Ridge to a fire tower and back.
Type of Trail: Rocky footpaths.
Distance: 4.7 miles
Hiking Time: 3 hours
Lowest Elevation: 1,000 feet
Highest Elevation: 1,340 feet
USGS Quad: Newfoundland
Other Maps: NYNJTC North Jersey Trails — Map #21, NWCDC map

The Pequannock River watershed area, managed by the Newark Watershed Conservation and Development Corporation (NWCDC), features an extensive trail network maintained by the New York-New Jersey Trail Conference. The watershed area — which includes the southern portion of Bearfort Mountain, a number of ponds and reservoirs, and a large portion of the wild highlands south of Wawayanda State Park — has geological significance because Clinton Road forms the divide between the Precambrian gneiss of the Highlands and the much younger Paleozoic strata of Bearfort Mountain. Due to the difference in the bedrock, two different kinds of mountain scenery are found here. The hike described below is on Bearfort Mountain, while the following one, Buckabear Pond, is in the Highlands.

The NWCDC requires you to have a permit to hike these trails, which presently costs $8.00 per year. They have established marked parking areas at trailheads and, when you purchase the permit, will provide you with a map (showing distances to the nearest tenth of a mile) and a car parking decal. You must pick up your permit in person on weekdays or on Saturday mornings at the NWCDC's office in Newfoundland, one mile north of N.J. Route 23 on Echo Lake Road (973-697-2850).

Trailhead: From N.J. Route 23, drive north 2.9 miles on Clinton Road to Parking Area #2. This is a small parking area located on the right-hand side of the road, large enough for two or three cars.

Directions: From the parking area, hike into the woods on the Fire Tower West Trail, a woods road marked with yellow blazes. After 350 feet, bear right onto a blue trail. Follow this trail for 0.35 mile through the woods, with some climbing, until the trail ends at a dirt road. Turn left on the road, following the red-and-white blazes of the Fire Tower Ridge Trail, and, after a short distance, you will reach the former site of Cross Castle, which was demolished in 1988. For many years, the stone walls of this old mansion were used as a beer-drinking sanctuary by the locals. Now, only a small part of one wall remains. The red-on-white markers continue through the castle site, then bear left, still following the woods road. To the right, through the trees, you will see Hanks Pond in the valley below. In another 500 feet, a road leads left to an old stone water tower. This interesting circular structure, which formerly served Cross Castle, is also visible from the trail.

Continue following the red-and-white blazes. In another 0.7

mile, the woods road turns left, uphill, and ends at a rock outcrop. The blazed trail bears right and continues as a footpath, following rock outcrops along swamps and through pine woods. This is a beautiful section of trail, marked primarily with white paint blazes on the rocks. After 0.3 mile, a blue-blazed trail joins from the right in a rocky cleft with an underground stream. The blue-blazed trail runs concurrently with the red-and-white trail for about a quarter of a mile, then bears left at a fork. Turn right here and continue along the red-and-white trail. In another 0.6 mile, you will emerge onto a lawn and picnic area, usually deserted, in front of the fire tower. The teal diamond-blazed Highlands Trail comes in from the north here and turns west at the tower.

After a visit to the tower, which is manned seasonally, with its tremendous views of the Bearfort Ridge and beyond, walk about 150 feet westward along the Highlands Trail and you will come to a woods road, the route of the yellow-blazed Fire Tower West Trail and of the Highlands Trail. Turn left and continue for about 100 feet, then bear right at a fork and continue on a footpath through the woods. You will come to a good viewpoint to the west in 0.2 mile, and about half a mile further, you will notice to the left the terminus of the blue-blazed trail that cuts across the ridge. Shortly thereafter, the white-blazed Two Brooks Trail bears off to the right and downhill. The Highlands Trail follows this white trail, but you should continue on the yellow-blazed trail, which takes the left fork. In another 1.3 miles, you will reach the end of the trail and your car.

14 Pequannock Watershed Buckabear Pond

> **General Description:** A moderate hike along a ridge to a hidden pond, with a few short ups-and-downs.
> **Type of Trail:** Rocky footpaths.
> **Distance:** 5.0 miles
> **Hiking Time:** 3.5 hours
> **Lowest Elevation:** 1,038 feet
> **Highest Elevation:** 1,263 feet
> **USGS Quad:** Newfoundland
> **Other Maps:** NYNJTC North Jersey Trails — Map #21, NWCDC map

Trailhead: From N.J. Route 23, drive north 4.5 miles on Clinton Road to Parking Area #4 (marked as "P4"), just past the bridge over Mossmans Brook.

Directions: From the parking area, walk south on Clinton Road for about 400 feet. Look for three white blazes on the right, which mark the beginning of the Clinton West Trail, and turn right onto a dirt road — also the route of the teal diamond-blazed Highlands Trail, which is co-aligned with the Clinton West Trail for the next few miles. You will pass through a hemlock grove and, in another 125 feet, turn right onto a footpath, following both white and teal diamond blazes. Soon, the trail turns sharp left and begins to climb. After ascending about 200 vertical feet to what appears to be the crest of the ridge, you will come to a junction, with the trail ahead marked with blue blazes. Turn left here, continuing to follow the white and teal diamond blazes. You are now heading south along a wooded ridge, loaded with mountain laurel and blueberry bushes.

In 0.8 mile, you will come to a limited viewpoint to the east from a rocky ridge, with Clinton Reservoir and the southern end of Bearfort Mountain visible. A quarter of a mile further along the trail — after passing a line of cliffs to the right — you will reach a better viewpoint (look for the Bearfort Fire Tower to the left). A short distance afterwards, the red-triangle-on-white Buckabear Pond Trail crosses. The Clinton West/Highlands Trail soon begins a steady ascent and, 2.1 miles from the start, reaches a high point at the southern end of the ridge, with good views from rocks to the left of the trail. Now the trail begins a steady descent and — almost imperceptibly — starts curving to the west and then to the north. In about a quarter of a mile, the trail begins to follow an old woods road, now narrowed to a footpath, and passes through a particularly dense stand of laurel. The body of water to the left is an arm of the Clinton Reservoir. Eventually, the trail comes down to the level of the reservoir and runs along it for 0.15 mile. This is a very beautiful stretch of trail.

At 2.9 miles from the start of the hike, you will reach another junction. Here, the red-triangle-on-white Buckabear Pond Trail ends. Our route turns left and crosses the outlet of Buckabear Pond, following the white and teal diamond blazes. Beaver activity in the area has raised the level of Buckabear Pond, and the crossing of the dam over the outlet can be very difficult in all but low-water conditions, and especially in the winter, when it may be icy. In order to avoid getting wet, you will have to stay to the extreme left of the dam. (If the crossing is too hazardous, you can return to your car by following the Buckabear Pond Trail for about half a mile up the ridge to its intersection with the Clinton West/Highlands Trail, then turn left and retrace your steps for 1.5 miles.)

When you arrive at the western end of the dam, turn right, leaving the Clinton West/Highlands Trail. You will now be following the yellow-blazed Bearfort Waters/Clinton Trail, an old woods road which runs along the shore of Buckabear Pond. However, because of the continuing beaver activity, which has flooded several sections of this trail, the first part of the trail has been relocated to higher ground. Upon rejoining the original trail route near the pond, you will notice a large rock along the shore. This is a nice place to stop for a few minutes and enjoy the scenery of this remote pond.

In another quarter of a mile, you will reach the inlet stream of the pond. The trail has been flooded where it crosses this stream, and you will want to go a little upstream of the blazed route, where the stream can be easily crossed on rocks. Soon afterwards, you will come to a flat area with a large rock overlooking the pond. Unfortunately, this spot is accessible from the west via a dirt road that can be negotiated by four-wheel drive vehicles, and it is a favorite site for local beer drinkers. The trash they often leave behind mars the beauty of this location.

North of here, the trail route may be submerged in the pond during wet seasons, requiring you to bushwhack further up the slope to the left. (Plans are underway to relocate the trail to higher ground.) Soon, you'll come to another flat area where an old blue car has been left to rust away. In the next 0.2 mile, you may encounter some more areas where the trail is submerged. Some of the bushwhacking required to avoid these locations can be rather difficult. Finally, the trail climbs to a high point overlooking the pond and then descends to reach the northern end of the pond. Here you will pass through a hemlock grove and cross the brook which feeds the pond. The trail now begins to climb the ridge and, in half a mile, reaches a junction with a blue-blazed trail. Turn right on the blue trail, and in 0.1 mile the blazes will turn to white/teal diamond at the point where you made a left turn earlier in the hike. After 0.25 mile downhill, you will reach Clinton Road. Turn left to Parking Area #4 and your car.

15 Wawayanda State Park

> **General Description:** A moderate hike along old roads and through deep forests and a cedar swamp.
> **Type of Trail:** Woods roads, with some wet sections; expect to see mountain bikes.
> **Distance:** 6.4 miles
> **Hiking Time:** 4 hours
> **Lowest Elevation:** 1,100 feet
> **Highest Elevation:** 1,280 feet
> **USGS Quad:** Wawayanda
> **Other Maps:** NYNJTC North Jersey Trails — Map #21, NJ Walk Book Map #19, DEP map

Before the 1980s, few trails were marked among the many woods roads that run through the swamps and rhododendron jungles of Wawayanda State Park. It was easy then to get lost and end up hiking a good distance further than intended. Today, however, the park has over 20 marked trails, including seven miles of the Appalachian Trail, affording the hiker the opportunity to enjoy a variety of interesting natural features within the park boundaries.

There are dramatic overlooks from Wawayanda Mountain, the Wawayanda Hemlock Ravine Natural Area, and Terrace Pond in the Bearfort Mountain Natural Area, but the real heartland of the park is traversed by the hike described below. Here, in the Wawayanda Swamp Natural Area, you will not have expansive views, but you will get a feeling of remoteness, almost wilderness, at certain points. On the other hand, as you hike next to heavily used Wawayanda Lake, or get passed by a mountain bike, you will be reminded that you are still in New Jersey.

Trailhead: From N.J. Route 23, take Union Valley Road (County Route 513) north into West Milford. Bear left at the shopping center (following the sign for Wawayanda and Upper Greenwood Lake) and left again at the Y intersection, and you will come to Warwick Turnpike. Make a left here, and head towards Upper Greenwood Lake. About 2.4 miles past your first glimpse of Upper Greenwood Lake, still on Warwick Turnpike, you will see the entrance to the park on your left. Pass the park office and continue out to the lake and its swimming/boating areas. Continue past the first parking area (adjacent to the swimming area) and park in the second parking area (for boating and fishing). An auxiliary entrance to the park, convenient for those coming from the west, can be reached via Wawayanda Road in Barry Lakes. This entrance is open Memorial Day through Labor Day.

During the summer season (Memorial Day through Labor Day), a fee of $5.00 on weekdays and $7.00 on weekends is charged (as of 2002). If you come during the summer and don't want to pay the fee, an option is to park for free at the lot north of the park office/visitor center and take the blue Hoeferlin Trail south to the yellow Double Pond Trail, turn right, do the loop described below and return the same way. This will add about four miles to the hike. The Hoeferlin Trail goes between the visitor center and the toll booths on the south side of the road. Other free options are as follows: (1) Park at the auxiliary entrance to the park and walk the quarter mile or so to the lake. (2) Park at the junction of Cherry

Ridge Road and the Banker Trail, which is accessible from Clinton Road at the north end of Lookover Lake. Although Cherry Ridge Road is unpaved, this spot is indicated as a parking area on NYNJTC Map #21, and it is located about halfway into the hike described below.

Directions: From the boating and fishing parking area at Wawayanda Lake, proceed east (left, when facing the lake) on a woods road which runs along the north shore of the lake to the dam, then continue straight ahead, away from the lake. You will soon reach the remains of the charcoal blast furnace, which will be on your left. Built in 1846, this furnace was used to smelt iron ore from local mines. It was part of Wawayanda Village, an industrial village that included the furnace, mines, mills, a school, charcoal-making works, a brick kiln and homes for workers. The historic Wawayanda Mule Barn, built in 1855, once stood here. This large stone-and-timber structure, the last structure of old Wawayanda Village to survive into the park era, was destroyed by fire in November 1985.

From the furnace, keep right and pick up the yellow-blazed Laurel Pond Trail, marked by a sign. This road was surveyed as a public road in 1811 and remained open to traffic until the mid-1920s. In another third of a mile, the beautiful spring-fed Laurel Pond will be visible through the trees, below on your right. After an unblazed side trail leaves to the right (it leads to a rocky overlook over the pond), the Laurel Pond Trail begins to climb. At the height of land, the blue-blazed Wingdam Trail goes off to the right. Here, to the left of the trail, there is a view of the Wawayanda Plateau from a rock ledge. Continue straight ahead on the Laurel Pond Trail, which now descends through deep woods, with interesting rock outcrops on either side of the trail. After a short climb, it reaches Cherry Ridge Road (gravel), which is closed to cars, but not to dirt bike traffic.

Turn left on Cherry Ridge Road, and descend steadily. After crossing a stream on a wooden bridge, you will come to a marked junction. (Ignore the unmarked trail which leaves to the left about 300 feet beyond the bridge.) The road leading straight ahead here is the Old Coal Trail, marked by three red blazes. Turn left at this junction and continue along the unmarked Cherry Ridge Road. Soon, the Red Dot Trail leaves to the left. Then, about 0.3 mile from the junction with the Old Coal Trail, the road crosses the inlet of a swamp, which is soon visible to the right. After crossing another stream, the trail continues through a dense rhododenron thicket.

About half a mile from the second stream crossing, you will come to a trail junction at a vehicle turnaround. You are now about halfway through the hike. Here, you should turn left onto the yellow-blazed Banker Trail. In less than half a mile, this trail leads to the blue-blazed Cedar Swamp Trail, which goes off to the left as the Banker Trail curves to the right. Continue ahead on the Cedar Swamp Trail.

The Cedar Swamp Trail is one of the most interesting trails in the park. Partially a cut footpath, it is unlike most of the other trails, which follow old roads. The Cedar Swamp Trail proceeds through dense growth of rhododendron, through seasonally wet areas, and past big hemlocks. At several points, the rhododendron is so dense that the trail actually tunnels under it! After about a mile, the trail reaches the amazing Cedar Swamp, with its unusual stand of tall, rare inland Atlantic white cedars growing in a very wet environment. For about 700 feet, it crosses the swamp on puncheons. This section can be difficult to navigate during wet weather. The trail then to climbs to higher ground and once more begins to follow a woods road.

About a third of a mile from the end of the swamp, the Cedar Swamp Trail terminates at the yellow-blazed Double Pond Trail, which comes in at a sharp angle from the right. Continue ahead on a woods road, now following the Double Pond Trail. You will pass the northern end of the Red Dot Trail to the left in 0.4 mile, and immediately afterwards the Double Pond Trail crosses another swamp on a wooden bridge and puncheons. A quarter of a mile beyond the swamp, the trail reaches a gate and passes by a group camping area to the left. After passing a sign marking the end of the Double Pond Trail and crossing a bridge over a stream, you will reach the furnace near Wawayanda Lake. Turn right at the furnace and retrace your steps, following the road along the shore of the lake back to your car.

16 Mahlon Dickerson Reservation

> **General Description:** An easy-to-moderate walk through deep forest and pine swamp, and over the highest point in Morris County.
>
> **Type of Trail:** Woods roads, with mountain bikes allowed.
>
> **Distance:** 4.1 miles
>
> **Hiking Time:** 2.5 hours
>
> **Lowest Elevation:** 1,150 feet
>
> **Highest Elevation:** 1,388 feet
>
> **USGS Quad:** Franklin
>
> **Other Maps:** Morris County Park Commission map

Mahlon Dickerson Reservation is named for a local citizen who, in the early nineteenth century, was elected Governor of New Jersey, served in the United States Senate, and became a United States District Court judge. The Reservation is large, over 3,200 acres in area, and seems to keep growing with additional land acquisitions. It is located in the wildest section of Morris County, where bear sightings are not uncommon. The Reservation offers miles of hiking on old woods roads and an old railroad bed, plus two camping areas.

The most dramatic feature in the hike described below is the change of vegetation. For most of the hike, you will pass through upland deciduous forest growth, with typical oak, maple, etc. But for about half a mile, the trail goes through the strikingly different Pine Swamp, with its extensive stands of spruce, rhododendron and native azalea. This is a very wet area, yet the trail is mainly on higher ground and can be walked without serious problems even during very wet periods. The trail is also, for nearly its entire length, on woods roads that are conducive to walking with a group. In addition, it makes an excellent cross-country ski route. There is only one significant climb along the route, making it a good bet for a first hike. If you would like to include an expansive view in your day of walking, check out the Headley Overlook, which is a short walk from the parking area and is well marked with signs.

Trailhead: Take Interstate Route 80 to Exit 34B, continue north for 5.0 miles on N.J. Route 15, and take the exit for Weldon Road and Milton. After about 1.5 miles on Weldon Road, you will pass a sign indicating that you have entered Mahlon Dickerson Reservation. Soon, you will pass the entrance to Saffin Pond on the right. Continue for another mile, and you will pass an entrance to a camping area on the left. Immediately afterward, you will pass another entrance on the right. Turn left at the next park entrance — this one, an entrance to a picnic area on the left — and continue ahead to the parking area.

Directions: Nearly the entire hike follows white blazes, but there are many turns, so pay close attention to the markings. For the first 1.4 miles, the route also follows the teal-blazed Highlands Trail.

The hike begins at the end of the parking area, at first following a service road marked with the teal diamond blazes of the Highlands Trail. You will pass a fitness station and a

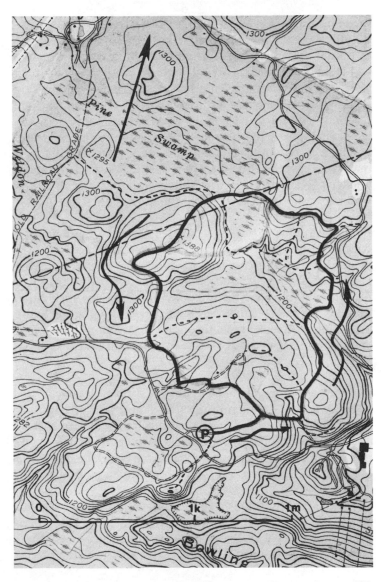

water pump, and in about 500 feet, the pavement ends. After 0.2 mile, you will reach a junction with the white-blazed Pine Swamp Circular Trail. Turn right (now following both white and teal blazes), head downhill across a brook, and then turn left. Continue along the Pine Swamp Circular Trail, making sure to follow the white and teal blazes at each intersection. In about two-thirds of a mile, you'll cross another brook. Soon afterwards, the blazed trail bears left at a fork, and you'll enter a mountain laurel thicket and encounter the first major wet area on this hike. Just past this swampy section, you'll reach a junction with a yellow trail that cuts off a little walking without missing any of the interesting scenery.

If you wish to take the longer way, turn right, following the white and teal markings, and cross a small brook and wet area. Soon you'll reach a trail junction near a road. Here, the Highlands Trail, with its teal blazes, leaves to the right, while the white-blazed Pine Swamp Circular Trail — which is the route of this hike — turns left. Continue following the white blazes for another 0.3 mile, through a dry woods, to the other end of the yellow trail. It is here that the real Pine Swamp is entered.

The Pine Swamp, crammed with tall spruce, hemlock, rhododendron and mountain laurel, is remote and gives a feeling of deep wilderness (unless an airplane happens to pass overhead). Wildlife is in abundance here. A good view of this interesting natural area may be had from a rocky ledge to the left, about 200 feet beyond the end of the yellow trail.

The white trail continues through the swamp, crosses a small brook, and ascends slightly to another junction. Here, bear left at the fork. The trail now climbs gradually to the highest point in Morris County (1,395 feet), marked by a sign placed by the Park Commission. (The actual high point is a short distance to the right of the trail.) From here, the trail descends, reaching a junction in about half a mile. Turn left at this junction, then left again in another 75 feet. The second turn marks the beginning of the green-blazed Boulder Trail, which runs concurrently with the white trail. This trail is named for the interesting large boulders which can be seen on both sides of the trail.

After half a mile along the green trail, the white blazes turn right onto a footpath — a welcome change from the woods roads that the trail has followed until now. The Pine Swamp Circular Trail soon rejoins another woods road and, after a few more turns, it arrives back at the start of the trail. Turn right and continue along the service road to the parking area and your car.

Saffin Pond

17 Allamuchy Mountain State Park

> **General Description:** An easy-to-moderate walk on old woods roads, past a pond and through deep woods.
> **Type of Trail:** Woods roads; expect mountain bikes and horses.
> **Distance:** 3.9 miles
> **Hiking Time:** 2 hours
> **Lowest Elevation:** 950 feet
> **Highest Elevation:** 1,060 feet
> **USGS Quad:** Tranquility
> **Other Maps:** DEP map

Allamuchy Mountain State Park is located on a high plateau in the Highlands that was farmed for a long time and is now in various stages of regrowth. There is an abundance of wildlife, and the walking, which is entirely on woods roads, is quite easy. There are several sections of the park, both north and south of I-80. The section used for this hike is the Allamuchy Natural Area, which contains 15 miles of trail — mostly old woods roads — that offer excellent cross-country skiing in the winter. As of this writing, the trails are poorly blazed, so follow the directions carefully. The park is managed through Stephens State Park (which offers car camping).

Trailhead: Take Interstate Route 80 to Exit 19, and continue south on County Route 517 towards Hackettstown for 2.1 miles (from the middle of the overpass over I-80). Turn left on Deer Park Road (next to a brick house and also marked by a wooden post), and follow this narrow paved road (which is in rather poor condition, including some potholes) for 0.7 mile to the official park entrance. Keep going along the road (which now becomes a dirt road, with a number of rough spots) and in another mile, shortly after passing a house, you will reach a gate and Parking Area #1. Continue for just over half a mile to another gate, this one closed, and park at Parking Area #2, which is to your left. (In winter, the gate across the road at Parking Area #1 may be closed. If so, park at Parking Area #1 and walk the extra distance.) Along the road between the two parking areas are signs which indicate the age of some abandoned fields, in various stages of succession. Some of the fields in this area are intentionally burned each year, in the early spring, to provide improved habitat for wildlife.

Directions: From the parking area, walk around the gate and head straight into the forest on a path. Do not follow the main dirt road, which turns to the right. Both routes are marked with white blazes, but be sure you are on the less traveled path. In about 200 feet from where the path leaves the road, another path (marked with red blazes) goes off to the left. Continue straight ahead, following the white markers. You will be heading gradually uphill, and in another 0.3 mile, you will reach a junction with another path. Make a right turn here and follow this path down to Deer Park Pond. (Although this trail is supposed to be marked red, there are no red blazes or markers until you reach the lake. A few circular red markers may be found along the shore of the lake.) Upon reaching the lake, which was once part of an estate, you will probably notice beaver activity in the area. The trail follows the northwestern shore and then swings around, passes an old stone foundation and some rock piles, and comes out on the opposite shore at a small clearing just before reaching a dense stand of tall evergreens.

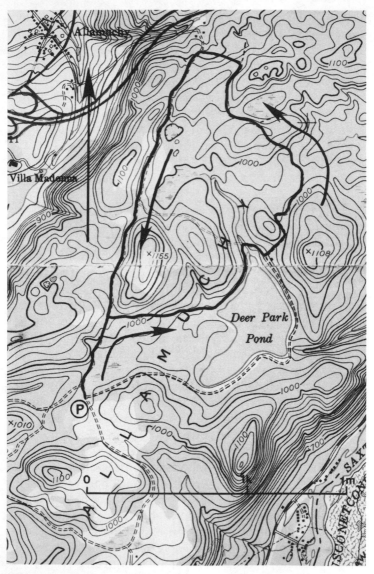

(*Shorter Hike:* For a hike of only two miles, turn right here and follow the lane around the pond and back through woods to the parking area. The path, marked with white blazes, is obvious and easy to follow.)

To continue with the longer circuit, make a left at this small clearing onto a trail that heads uphill. There are no blazes at the junction, but after the trail climbs a little and turns left, it begins to be marked with both blue and white blazes. The trail then begins to descend, reaching an intersection at a low area in about 0.4 mile. Here the blue trail leaves to the right. Follow the white markers to the left, crossing the outlet of a small swamp, and begin a gradual climb through rocky woods. The trail then levels off, and just after it curves to the right, you'll come to another junction. Make a left, still following the white markers. The trail begins to descend and crosses two old rock walls, with the access roads leading to the Route 80 scenic overlook visible to the right when the leaves are down. Just past the point where the trail begins to head south, look for a well-used footpath that passes through an opening in a fence. Turn right and follow it for about 200 yards to the scenic overlook, with a fine view of the Kittatinny Mountains and the Delaware Water Gap.

Return to the main trail, which now heads southwest, and begin to descend, soon passing a large overhanging boulder to the left. After climbing a little, you will pass through areas where fields are reverting to woods — a transitional forest. After about a mile of walking, still following white markers, you will reach the junction where you turned off the white trail on the way in. Continue straight ahead, and in another 0.4 mile you will reach the starting point and your car. About halfway back, a faint trail veers off to the left (at a tree with white metal blazes) and climbs a small hill (no views), which again is part woods and part overgrown field.

18 Hacklebarney State Park

General Description: An easy-to-moderate walk down to a scenic river in a hemlock ravine.
Type of Trail: Woods roads and footpaths, some rocky and indistinct.
Distance: 2.8 miles
Hiking Time: 2 hours
Lowest Elevation: 440 feet
Highest Elevation: 680 feet
USGS Quad: Gladstone
Other Maps: DEP map

This short hike will lead you through some little-used and very beautiful areas of a heavily-used state park. Don't come here on a weekend in the summer unless you like crowds. It's a developed park, with large restrooms, a playground, and the densest concentration of picnic tables in a hemlock gorge you'll probably ever see. There are also a number of ancient, non-functioning water fountains in the most unlikely places. There is a network of trails, but they are not marked, although a map is available at the headquarters. Some of these trails are fire roads, some are footpaths and others are gravel-covered walkways.

Trailhead: From the intersection of U.S. Route 206 and County Route 513 (also designated as N.J. Route 24) in Chester, proceed west on County Route 513 for 1.3 miles, passing the entrance to Cooper Mill County Park on the left. Continue ahead for another 0.1 mile and turn left at a brown-and-yellow state park sign, then make another sharp left onto State Park Road. Follow this road, with the Black River on your left, for 1.8 miles, and bear right where the road continues straight ahead unpaved. In another 0.6 mile, you will come to the entrance to the park on your left. Follow the entrance road for 0.2 mile to the main parking area.

Directions: From the main parking area, backtrack towards the park entrance until you see a "Smoky the Bear" sign on the left. Turn sharply left here onto a gravel lane which heads uphill, with a gate blocking access to all but authorized vehi-

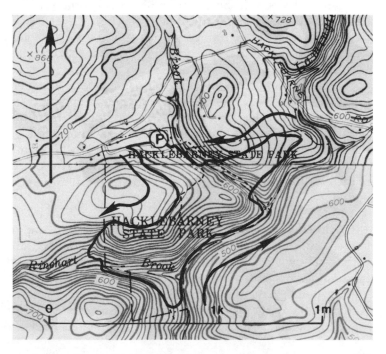

cles. In another 350 feet, you will reach a fork in the road. Bear left and continue along the gravel road, which now levels off. Soon you will pass a sign to the right that marks a side trail to an "overlook." The trail leads in 350 feet to a wooden observation platform, with limited views over the countryside. Although this viewpoint could hardly be characterized as spectacular, it is the only one in the park.

After about a third of a mile on the gravel lane, you will reach a clearing, with playground equipment on the right. Continue through the clearing, then turn right onto a footpath that passes in front of two park benches (not the gravel road that goes behind the benches). You will soon enter a natural area of deep woods. The trail climbs briefly, then descends gradually along the side of the hill. Towards the base of the descent, the trail goes down stone steps, curving sharply to the left, and begins to run along Rhinehart Brook.

Soon you will come to a junction, with an abandoned water fountain to the left. Turn right here, crossing the brook on a wide wooden bridge, then bear left, and follow the trail uphill, with the brook to your left. After descending slightly, the trail reaches a **T** junction. Bear left at this junction, and continue downhill to the Black River. (To the right, the other branch of the trail leads in a short distance to the park boundary, marked by two stone pillars.)

After crossing a wooden bridge over a small tributary and a longer footbridge over Rhinehart Brook, the graded trail ends, and the hike continues on a narrow, rocky and (at times) indistinct footpath. This is quite a contrast to the wide, graded paths that you have been following up to now. Although the route may be less than obvious at times, you are following along the bank of the river, so there is no danger of getting lost. This remote section of the park is particularly beautiful, with massive boulders, falls and rapids. Soon after passing a very large boulder in the river, you will notice a gravel road which descends to the river level. The trail soon joins this road, providing a welcome respite from the rock-hopping, but in 500 feet (after passing another abandoned water fountain and a number of picnic tables), the road ends, and the trail again becomes a rocky footpath. (It should be noted that the property on the opposite side of the river is privately owned, and hunting is allowed there in season.)

After following the river for about half a mile from the footbridge over Rhinehart Brook, you will reach a large group of picnic tables at a clearing, with a small restroom building to the left. The trail joins a gravel road which curves left, soon reaching a footbridge which crosses Trout Brook. Do not cross this bridge; rather, continue ahead, parallel to the brook, for 100 feet and turn right onto a footpath that passes a picnic table and leads to another footbridge over the creek. Cross this bridge and continue ahead through a rocky area. In a short distance, you will see a rocky path which heads to the right. Follow this path, which curves to the left and in 100 feet passes another abandoned water fountain. Now the path becomes wider and smoother, and it goes through a forest of huge, stately hemlocks high above the Black River.

In about 0.3 mile, the trail swings left and meets a gravel fire road. Turn left here, and follow this road for a third of a mile until you reach another bridge over Trout Brook. Here you have two options. You can turn left, cross the bridge, then turn right, keeping to the right at the next intersection, and continue walking uphill to reach the parking area. An alternative is to continue straight ahead along the east side of the brook up to another bridge, cross it, climb the stairs and turn right onto the road to reach the parking area.

19 Jenny Jump State Forest

> **General Description:** An easy walk, with a short climb through woods to two excellent overlooks. Good for children, but be careful at the overlooks.
> **Type of Trail:** Footpaths and woods roads.
> **Distance:** 1.4 miles
> **Hiking Time:** 1 hour
> **Lowest Elevation:** 940 feet
> **Highest Elevation:** 1,080 feet
> **USGS Quad:** Blairstown
> **Other Maps:** DEP map

Jenny Jump State Forest, located near Route 80 in Warren County, features mountainous terrain with several excellent views. The name of the forest comes from a legend recorded by a Swedish missionary in 1747. According to one version of the legend, Jenny Lee, the daughter of a European settler, jumped off the ridge in an attempt to escape from approaching Indians. The 2,014-acre forest is very popular with car campers, and there are also eight cabins that can be rented. The hike traverses a mountaintop area where the temperatures are normally a little cooler than in surrounding areas.

Although the hike described below is the shortest one in the book, it is a very interesting walk which includes several outstanding vistas. A longer hike of about three miles, using the Spring, Summit and Orchard Trails, is also possible. Hiking trail maps can be obtained at the park office.

Trailhead: *Take Interstate Route 80 to Exit 12. Proceed south on County Route 521 for 1.1 miles to the center of Hope, and turn left on County Route 519. In 1.1 miles, just before a pond, turn right onto Shiloh Road (this turn, as well as all subsequent turns, is marked with a yellow-and-brown park sign). You will reach a fork at 1.1 miles; turn right onto State Park Road, a narrow, twisting road, which proceeds uphill. In 0.8 mile, you will pass a park entrance sign. Proceed for another 0.2 mile, turn left and continue several hundred feet to the forest office and visitors' parking area. Bear right and proceed for another 0.1 mile to a small parking area opposite a restroom building. (In winter, this parking area may be closed, and you should park at the visitors' parking area next to the office.)*

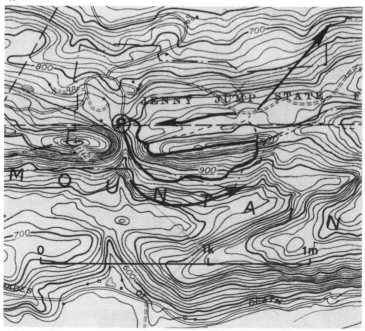

From the parking area, proceed ahead on the paved road, which curves to the right. You will pass a sign marking the trailhead of the Summit and Swamp Trails, and go by another parking area on the right. Continue beyond this parking area (where the paving ends), and in another 200 feet a sign will mark the start of the blue-blazed Spring Trail. After skirting an open area to the left, the trail runs near the edge of a rocky ravine on the right, with some nice views into the ravine. It then swings left and continues for about half a mile on a relatively level path. At 0.7 mile, soon after passing some rocky cliffs on the left, the trail turns left and begins a strenuous, though relatively short, climb uphill.

At the top of the rise, you will come to a junction with the yellow-blazed Summit Trail. Turn left and follow the yellow markers, which lead to the ridge of Jenny Jump Mountain, with views to the north and south. After walking along the summit ridge for about 0.2 mile, you will notice two interesting glacial erratics in an open area. The one on the right is formed of sandstone, which is very different from the underlying bedrock. About 100 feet further along the trail, a side trail leads left to a magnificent viewpoint. The vista from this overlook includes both forest and the highly fertile fields of the Great Valley.

The yellow trail now widens into a woods road and, in 0.2 mile, turns right and begins a steady descent. Just beyond this turn, a side trail leads left over bare granite bedrock (with glacial striations) to another viewpoint, with the Pinnacle directly ahead and the Delaware Water Gap in the distance to the right (west). The trail continues to descend, and the red-blazed Swamp Trail soon joins from the right. After skirting Campsite #9, the joint red and yellow trails bear left, pass two cabins, and end at the parking area.

The Ridge and Valley Province

20 High Point State Park

General Description: A long but moderate hike along a scenic section of the Appalachian Trail, with a return via old woods roads that pass near a lake.
Type of Trail: Rocky footpaths and woods roads.
Distance: 6.4 miles
Hiking Time: 4 hours
Lowest Elevation: 1,320 feet
Highest Elevation: 1,630 feet
USGS Quad: Port Jervis South
Other Maps: NYNJTC Kittatinny Trails — Map #18, NJ Walk Book Map #18, DEP High Point State Park map

---

High Point State Park, particularly the section north of Route 23, is very popular with picnickers and casual hikers. Here is the famed High Point monument, which commemorates New Jersey citizens who fought in our country's wars. This 220-foot obelisk marks the highest point in the roughly 50-mile ridge line of Kittatinny Mountain, and it is visible from nearly every northwestern New Jersey summit viewpoint. Just to the northeast of the monument lies New Jersey's first natural area, the 800-acre Dryden Kuser Natural Area, which contains a virgin cedar swamp. Also nearby is Lake Marcia, developed for swimming. From Memorial Day to Labor Day, entrance to this section of High Point State Park is by fee ($5.00 weekdays, $7.00 weekends).

The section of High Point State Park south of Route 23 is unlike the intensively developed section described above. Relatively few people visit the area, and access is free. Here is a large tract of near wilderness, with rocky outcrops and hidden swamps, traversed by the Appalachian Trail (A.T.). There are two overnight shelters in this area, one of which — the Rutherford Shelter — is the most remote A.T. shelter in New Jersey.

Trailhead: Take N.J. Route 23 to High Point, and park in the designated Appalachian Trail parking area, which is about 200 feet east of the park office on the south side of the highway. The parking area itself is hidden from the road. Overnight parking requires a permit which can be obtained at the park office.

Directions: From the southwest corner of the A.T. parking area, follow an unmarked footpath for 100 feet and turn left on the white-blazed Appalachian Trail, here also marked with the yellow-on-white blazes of the Mashipacong Trail. In 0.1 mile, you will reach a trail junction, with a painted drainage pipe to the left rising vertically from the ground to a height of about four feet. The A.T. continues straight ahead, the red-on-white-blazed Iris Trail is to your left, and the yellow-on-white-blazed Mashipacong Trail goes off to your right. Continue on the white-blazed A.T. straight ahead through the woods, and ascend gradually to the main ridge. The trail continues south over jagged rocks. After about a mile, the Blue Dot Trail leaves to the right (it leads down to Sawmill Lake), and a short distance beyond, you'll reach a viewpoint to the west over the lake.

After about a mile and a half of walking, some views to the east appear, and Lake Rutherford, a reservoir for the

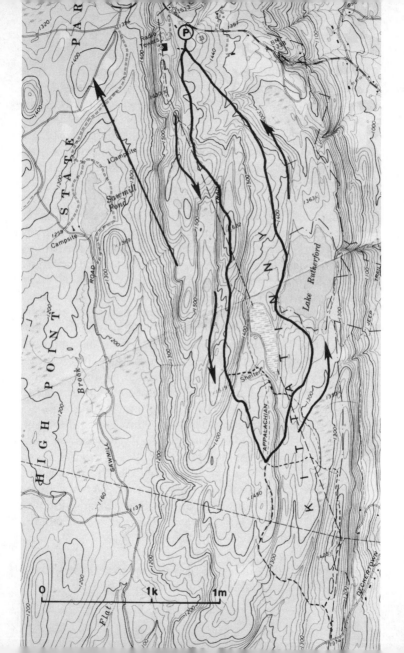

Borough of Sussex, becomes a prominent feature. Then, 2.3 miles from the start, you will reach an area where a large expanse of glacially scraped rock to the left of the trail provides excellent views eastward. After passing a few more viewpoints from exposed rocks, a blue-blazed trail to the left leads downhill to the Rutherford Shelter and a spring. If you are backpacking, this shelter is where you will want to set up camp. (There are several adjacent tent sites if the shelter itself is occupied.)

Continuing on the A.T. heading south, you will come (in another 0.8 mile) to the intersection of the A.T. and the Iris Trail. Turn left here and follow the red-on-white blazes of the Iris Trail through deep woods. The Iris Trail, an old woods road, is easy walking, with no difficult climbs, and it can be a great relief after three miles on jagged rock. In three-quarters of a mile, you will come to a junction with another woods road. Turn left here, staying on the Iris Trail, then bear right at the next fork. Not far from this turn, the Iris Trail begins to run along the west shore of Lake Rutherford. Several rock outcrops along the shore of this lake make good rest stops. Swimming is not permitted, however, since the lake serves a municipal water supply. After another mile and a half, you will arrive at the junction with the A.T. that you encountered near the start of the hike. Turn right here and head back to your car at the parking area.

Shorter Hike: When you reach the junction with the blue-blazed trail leading to the Rutherford Shelter, turn left and follow the blue trail down to the shelter. Continue past the privy and out to the Iris Trail on the woods road that serves as access to the shelter. Turn left and head back to your car via the red-on-white-blazed Iris Trail, as described above. This will shorten your hike by over a mile. You'll also pass a spring and get to visit the shelter, which is located on the site of an old farm, with lilac bushes blooming in season.

Longer Hike: For a longer and more strenuous hike (2.4 extra miles), you can do a second loop utilizing the Iris Trail and the A.T. It is best, however, to alternate trails for variety and foot relief. At the intersection of the A.T. and the Iris Trail, instead of turning left on the Iris Trail and heading back to the parking area, turn right on the Iris Trail and continue ahead when the A.T. leaves to the left after about 350 feet. Follow the Iris Trail past the gas line cut, downhill and over a brook to its second junction with the A.T., again marked with a post. Now turning left on the A.T., head north, passing through typical Kittatinny ridge growth (scrub oak, heath, and pitch pines) to the gas line cut (which offers good views to the east). Go back down through a low area, and finally reconnect with the Iris Trail. Turn right, and return to your car via the Iris Trail, as described in the main hike.

View from the Kittatinny Ridge

21 Stony Brook Firetower Circular

General Description: A moderate hike, with some climbing, along a brook and up to a high ridge.
Type of Trail: Woods roads and rocky footpaths.
Distance: 4 miles
Hiking Time: 3 hours
Lowest Elevation: 900 feet
Highest Elevation: 1,500 feet
USGS Quad: Culvers Gap
Other Maps: NYNJTC Kittatinny Trails — Map #17, NJ Walk Book Map #17, DEP map

Stokes State Forest contains 15,000 acres of woodland on the Kittatinny ridge north and south of U.S. Route 206. Two of the most scenic features of the forest are Sunrise Mountain, providing fine views in several directions, and Tillman Ravine, a deep hemlock and rhododendron gorge. Both areas have been developed by the State to provide easy access, and they attract many visitors. Wildlife abounds in Stokes State Forest, and sightings of bear and wild turkey are common. The Appalachian Trail (A.T.) traverses the length of the forest, and there are a number of marked trails, which are mostly former farm and logging roads. Trailheads are generally marked with posts that designate permitted uses, and trails are blazed with painted dots or sheet metal strips nailed to trees (except for the A.T., which is marked with white paint). The hike described below utilizes a combination of old farm and logging roads and a section of the A.T. The next hike, Buttermilk Falls/Tillman Ravine/Blue Mountain Circular (Hike #22), takes you up Tillman Ravine.

*Trailhead: From U.S. Route 206 just west of Kittatinny Lake, enter Stokes State Forest (on your right) and proceed to the forest office, where you may obtain maps and other information. Between Memorial Day and Labor Day, a day-use fee is charged to enter the forest ($5 per car on weekdays, and $7 on weekends in 2002). From the forest office, follow signs to Stony Lake. At a **T** junction just under two miles ahead, turn right and continue another 0.3 mile to the large Stony Lake parking area. Five trails start near the information directory located on the east side of this lot. Bicycles are allowed on some of these trails, but not on others. Most of the hike described below follows paths for hikers only.*

Directions: Starting from the information directory (take a good look at the trail information on display), begin your hike by following a woods road which is blocked to motor vehicles by a gate. The first third of this hike utilizes the brown-blazed Stony Brook Trail, but pay close attention, since five trails (light green, green, brown, blue and red) initially utilize the same route. Soon you will see the red-blazed Swenson Trail veer off to the left, and in another 200 feet, the light-green-blazed Station Trail does the same. At the next intersection (about 375 feet further along on the trail), the blue-blazed Coursen Trail goes right, while the brown-blazed Stony Brook Trail and the dark-green-blazed Tower Trail bear left. Take the left fork, and continue along the brown trail, which runs between a rocky embankment and a spruce/red pine woods on the left and a wetland on the right. About half a mile from the start, the Tower Trail turns

off to the right, and in another 200 feet, the light-green Station Trail comes in from the left. Here there is a signpost for the Stony Brook Trail, and from now on you should see only brown blazes.

Continue straight ahead on the Stony Brook Trail (bicycles are not permitted on this trail), which follows an old farm road, passing evidence of former settlement and farming.

The trail can be wet in places. In about 0.3 mile, the trail turns right, crosses two small brooks, and begins a gradual climb, with Stony Brook on the right. The climb becomes steeper, and soon after passing a small cascade over a flat rock, you'll reach Sunrise Mountain Road. Cross the road and continue to follow the brown blazes for another 0.2 mile, until you reach a small clearing and trail junction. A left turn here onto the blue-blazed trail will take you to the Gren Anderson Shelter, originally built by the Green Mountain Club in 1958 and refurbished in 1994, but you should continue ahead a short distance to the end of the Stony Brook Trail at a junction with the white-blazed Appalachian Trail. Turn right (south) and follow the A.T. (again, bicycles are not permitted on this trail) for about a mile over rough rocks, first crossing the headwaters of Stony Brook, then gradually climbing until you reach a junction with the dark-green-blazed Tower Trail at a trail register. Continue on the A.T. for another 300 feet to open ledges and the Culver Fire Tower (also known as the Normanook Lookout Tower). Nearby is also a newer communications tower. From the fire tower, there are excellent views to the west and north. Below you is Stony Lake. Camelback Mountain and its ski area is visible far to your left in the west, and High Point and the distant Catskill Mountains can be seen to the northeast.

Now backtrack to the Tower Trail, turn left, and descend steeply over ledges (be careful here) to Sunrise Mountain Road. Cross the road, continuing to follow the green markers of the Tower Trail (bicycles permitted), for another 0.7 mile to a junction with the brown-blazed Stony Brook Trail. Turn left and follow the brown markers for about half a mile to the information directory at Stony Lake and the parking area.

22

General Description: A challenging and strenuous hike up and down ravines and over three summits.
Type of Trail: Gravel roads, woods roads and rocky footpaths.
Distance: 10 miles
Hiking Time: 7 hours
Lowest Elevation: 450 feet
Highest Elevation: 1,500 feet
USGS Quad: Dingmans Ferry 15'
Other Maps: NYNJTC Kittatinny Trails — Map #17, NJ Walk Book Map #17

At the southern end of Stokes State Forest is a scenic section of the Appalachian Trail that extends into the Delaware Water Gap National Recreation Area. For about four miles, the trail follows open ridges, with several expansive views to the west over the Delaware River and the Pocono Plateau. The hike begins by climbing through Tillman Ravine, a classic Kittatinny hemlock ravine, with several cascades, and it ends at Buttermilk Falls, which is most spectacular in the spring or after a rain. It is one of the most strenuous hikes in the book, with a total elevation gain of over 1,500 feet.

Trailhead: *Take U.S. Route 206 for 0.3 mile past the turnoff to the Stokes State Forest Office and turn south on Strubel Road.*

Continue for about four miles to Brink Road, make a right, and travel another mile past the parking areas for Tillman Ravine to an intersection near a cemetery. Make a left here onto dirt Mountain Road and continue for two miles to Buttermilk Falls. Immediately opposite the falls is a large parking area. Leave your car here. (Note: During the winter, Brink Road may be closed. An alternate route is to continue along Route 206 to Tuttles Corner and turn left onto County Route 521, then turn left onto Route 615 and follow it to Wallpack Center. A left turn here will lead to the intersection with Mountain Road near the cemetery mentioned above, where you should turn right to reach the Buttermilk Falls parking area.)

Directions: Retrace your steps along Mountain Road heading north, toward the cemetery you passed two miles back. The walk along this little-used road is pleasant, with attractive views of the surrounding farms. In about 40 minutes, just before you reach the cemetery, the road crosses Tillman Brook on a concrete bridge. Turn right here, leaving the road, and enter the woods on the north side of the brook, following an unmarked trail. Proceed upstream along the brook, keeping it to your right. The trail may be faint in places, but you can't get lost if you stay close to the brook.

In about half a mile, after some climbing, you will reach the most dramatic section of this magnificent hemlock and rhododendron ravine. You will notice a red-blazed trail that joins from the left. Continue along the stream, now following the red blazes. Soon, the trail will cross the brook five times on wooden bridges. After the fifth bridge, follow the red-blazed trail as it heads away from the stream and out to the upper Tillman Ravine parking area at paved Brink Road, then turn right and follow the road. In a quarter mile, the pavement swings left, but Brink Road continues ahead as a gravel road. Follow the gravel road for about a mile. You will

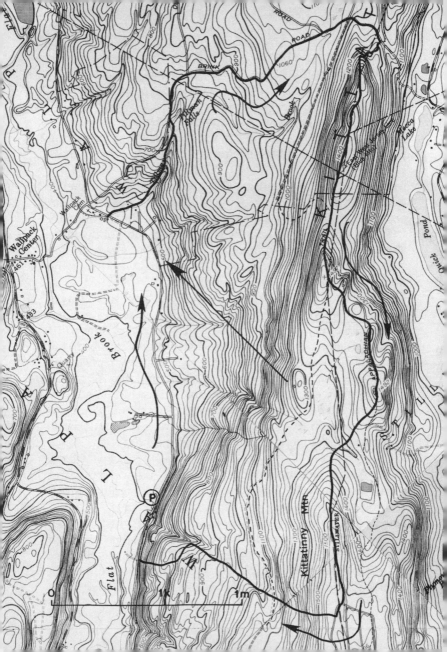

pass an intersection with Shay Road, which comes in from the left, and — after crossing Tillman Brook — reach a junction with Woods Road, where cars may be parked along the shoulder. Continue ahead on Brink Road, which is now blocked by a large boulder. In another 500 feet, you will pass the Brink Road Shelter to the left. There is a good spring about 300 feet behind the shelter on a blue-blazed side trail.

Continue on Brink Road for about 0.2 mile past the shelter and you will meet the white-blazed Appalachian Trail. Turn right (south) here, and begin your ascent of Blue Mountain. In 0.7 mile, after a moderately strenuous climb (followed by a short descent), you will emerge on the open ledges of Blue Mountain, with an excellent view to the west over the Delaware Valley and the Pocono Plateau in Pennsylvania. Continue heading south on the A.T., which soon leaves Stokes State Forest and enters the Delaware Water Gap National Recreation Area. Here, the A.T. turns left onto a dirt road that comes up from the west. The dirt road climbs to the top of Bird Mountain, where a short unmarked path to the right leads to another viewpoint. Just beyond, the A.T. turns left, leaving the dirt road, and begins to descend on a rocky footpath. After crossing a stream on rocks, the trail climbs to a rock outcrop that marks the summit of Rattlesnake Mountain (1,492 feet), with more views to the west.

From the summit, the trail descends, first rather steeply, and then more gradually. In 0.4 mile, it enters a hemlock grove and swings to the left to cross a stream on logs. (A blue-blazed trail to the left leads to a water source.) Just beyond, the trail turns left at a **T** intersection and begins to climb again. About half a mile after the stream crossing, as the trail bears left near the crest of the ridge, an unmarked trail to the right leads to a viewpoint to the west from slanted rock slabs, with pitch pine growing out of cracks in the rocks. This is an interesting contrast with the previous viewpoints and should not be missed.

The A.T. now levels off and, in another two-thirds of a mile, joins a gravel road that comes in from the left. This road was built as part of a planned second-home development that was abandoned when the Delaware Water Gap National Recreation area was created. About a quarter of a mile ahead, a short side trail on the right leads to the site of a former home. Just beyond, turn right on the blue-blazed Buttermilk Falls Trail, which begins here. (The Buttermilk Falls Trail can also be accessed from the far end of the homesite.) This trail descends in 1.6 miles to the base of the falls on Mountain Road, where you parked your car. It soon reaches a viewpoint to the west and, in half a mile, crosses the unmarked Woods Road Trail. As the trail nears the top of the falls, the grade steepens. Just above the falls, the trail crosses a wooden bridge which leads to a viewing platform. From here, the trail descends a series of stairways and walkways recently constructed to enable visitors to safely reach the top of the falls from the road.

Tillman Ravine

23 Blue Mountain Lake

General Description: A moderate hike to a remote mountain pond and a striking vista on the main Kittatinny ridge.

Type of Trail: Wide dirt and gravel roads; expect mountain bikes.

Distance: 5 miles

Hiking Time: 3 hours

Lowest Elevation: 1,100 feet

Highest Elevation: 1,250 feet

USGS Quad: Flatbrookville/Dingmans Ferry

Other Maps: NYNJTC Kittatinny Trails — Map #16, NJ Walk Book Map #16, Delaware Water Gap National Recreation Area Cross-Country Ski map

The Blue Mountain Lake section of the Delaware Water Gap National Recreation Area contains a large number of dirt roads. The remains of what was once to be a residential development, some of these roads have remnants of pavement in places. These roads parallel each other on either side of Blue Mountain Lake and extend a mile further to Hemlock Pond. In some sections, the remains of former homesites are visible. This complex of roads is shown on the map, which was last updated by aerial photography in 1971. You will also see the remains of an additional lake to the north of Blue Mountain Lake. This lake was drained in 1995. Because the

trails are all former roads, and there are numerous ups and downs, this area makes for excellent hiking, cross-country skiing and mountain biking, activities that the National Park Service supports and encourages. In fact, virtually the entire hike follows the route of the Blue Mountain Lake Mountain Bike Trail, which is marked at the various intersections by brown fiberglass wands with hiker, biker and skier symbols and arrows indicating the trail.

Trailhead: *Getting to the Blue Mountain Lake area will probably mean going there indirectly. Perhaps the most direct way is through Blairstown. From Route 94 in Blairstown, take County Route 602 west. When you reach the stop sign at the top of the hill above the church, make a sharp right and then bear left, staying on Route 602. Continue up and over the Kittatinny ridge and down into Millbrook Village. Bear right here and drive 1.5 miles north to a large white house (where snacks and refreshments may be available). Turn right here, following the sign for Blue Mountain Lake. The parking area is 1.3 miles ahead on the left.*

An alternative is to take Old Mine Road north from I-80 in the Delaware Water Gap. To reach this road, take the last exit in New Jersey and drive north, following signs to Millbrook Village, then bear left at the Millbrook intersection. The turnoff for Blue Mountain Lake is 1.5 miles past the village, at the large white house.

You can also take U.S. Route 206 past the Stokes State Forest headquarters and follow signs to Peter's Valley and the Wallpack Inn, first following County Route 521 and then County Route 615. Pass the Wallpack Inn and stay on Route 615, now following signs to Flatbrookville and Blairstown for another 6 miles. Turn left on a small bridge over the Flat Brook, leaving Route 615. Follow the road uphill from the bridge and make the first left, at the large white house, which will lead to the Blue Mountain Lake parking area on the left.

Directions: From the northeast end of the parking area, near the directory, follow the road for only 40 feet or so and turn right on a footpath heading downhill. Continue straight ahead where the trail joins a road which comes in from the right. Keep right at the clearing, where the gravel road climbs a little and then parallels the lake below it on the left. For the next half mile you'll pass many places along the shore of the lake that you may wish to explore. After going for about a mile, you will come to a junction where the trail splits (the arrows on the brown wand point in both directions). One branch heads straight ahead (use this one for a shorter hike — see below); the other turns right. Make a right here and head uphill until you reach a **T** intersection.

Make a left at the intersection and begin a long walk down and then steadily uphill. The lane you are on is shaded with oak, birch and maple, with an understory of mountain laurel and blueberry bushes. After the trail levels off and then descends slightly, you'll pass a swamp with signs of former beaver activity. You'll then reach a point where the road swings to the left and out to another **T** intersection. Turn left again, and immediately look for a path on the right that leads to Hemlock Pond. This pond is remarkable in that its entire shoreline is dominated by evergreens, an unusual sight in this part of New Jersey. It looks very much like a New England mountain pond. After your visit to this beautiful place, return to the main path and turn right, continuing up and then downhill until you come to a junction. A right turn here will lead in 100 yards to another view of Hemlock Pond, this one from its dam.

After returning from the pond, make a right at the junction and walk about another mile through a corridor of young black birch. For part of the way, you will notice a wall of boulders to the left. After passing a lane on the right, you will arrive at a fork in the road. A right turn here will lead in about 100 yards to a footpath on the right leading up to slabs of glacially polished bedrock. Walk over the rock and feel your way out toward an excellent vista. The Delaware River Valley and the Pocono Plateau, including Camelback Mountain, are in front of you. This rocky lookout, with stunted pitch pines, is called Indian Rocks. To continue the hike, return to the fork in the road, walk less than 100 feet, and turn left and downhill on a side trail. When you reach the bottom, turn right and follow this road, past evidence of former residences and along the two lakes (the first one having been drained). After about a mile, you will come to a junction near where you began the hike. Turn right on the footpath, which takes you to the parking area and your car.

Shorter Hike: A shorter version of this hike, about 2.5 miles in length, begins as described above, but continues straight ahead at the junction where you are directed in the above text to turn right and head uphill. From this point, follow the road as it winds around Blue Mountain Lake (as well as the former lake) through a low and wet area. At the top of a hill, where the road begins heading back towards the start of the hike, look for a path on the right that heads uphill. If you follow this up to a road, turn right for 100 feet, and then make a left, Indian Rocks will be on your right not far ahead. Walk out over the rocks to the viewpoint, then retrace your steps back down to the road that encircles the lake and turn right. The former lake and Blue Mountain Lake will be on your left, and you'll reach your car in about a mile.

24 Coppermines and Mt. Mohican

General Description: A moderately strenuous hike up a spectacular hemlock-and-rhododendron ravine and a walk along the crest of the Kittatinny Ridge to the summit of Mt. Mohican.
Type of Trail: Footpaths and woods roads.
Distance: 7.5 miles
Hiking Time: 4-5 hours
Lowest Elevation: 340 feet
Highest Elevation: 1,540 feet
USGS Quad: Portland, Bushkill
Other Maps: NYNJTC Kittatinny Trails — Maps #15 and #16; NJ Walk Book Maps #15 and #16

Although this hike climbs a good deal (the vertical rise is about 1,200 feet), the most strenuous part occurs during the first mile, in a spectacular hemlock ravine. The sights of cascades, waterfalls, dense rhododendrons and tall hemlocks are ample compensation for the work needed to traverse this section. The section of the Appalachian Trail utilized is a particularly scenic one, offering many views. This hike is accessed from the Old Mine Road, which dates back at least to the 1700s and probably began as an Indian trail.

The Coppermines Trail is named for the copper mines located in this area. There is evidence that the Dutch explored the area for copper in the 1600s, and a copper mine was first opened by John Redding in the mid-1700s. The last commercial mining venture in the area was by the Allegheny Mining Company in the early 1900s. None of these attempts to mine copper were commercially successful.

Trailhead: *Take Interstate Route 80 to the Delaware Water Gap, get off at the last exit in New Jersey, and head north along the Delaware River. The road is only one lane wide for about half a mile, and a special traffic light has been installed to regulate the two-way traffic. The Coppermine Parking Area is on the left, about 7.5 miles north of I-80. Park here and walk across the road to the trailhead.*

Directions: From the trailhead, follow the red markings of the Coppermines Trail uphill. Just past the trailhead, a trail to the left leads to the lower mine. Continue ahead, passing the ruins of a stone building to the left — the remnants of a mill that was built in the 1800s to process the copper ore. After 0.2 mile, a branch of the blue-blazed Kaiser Trail leaves to the right. Continue ahead on the red-blazed Coppermines Trail. In another 400 feet, the barricaded entrance to the upper mine is to the right of the trail. The trail now heads into the heart of a beautiful hemlock gorge. After crossing the brook on a wooden bridge, the trail begins to climb again. It ascends a switchback and then follows directly along the gorge. The magnificent gorge, with its hemlocks and rhododendron and its series of waterfalls, is below on the right. Finally, just beyond the end of the gorge, another blue-blazed trail leaves to the right. This trail will be your return route. Continue along the red-blazed Coppermines Trail as it levels off, crosses the brook again, and proceeds through a more open woods, typical of the Kittatinny upland. There may be some seasonally wet areas here. About two miles from the

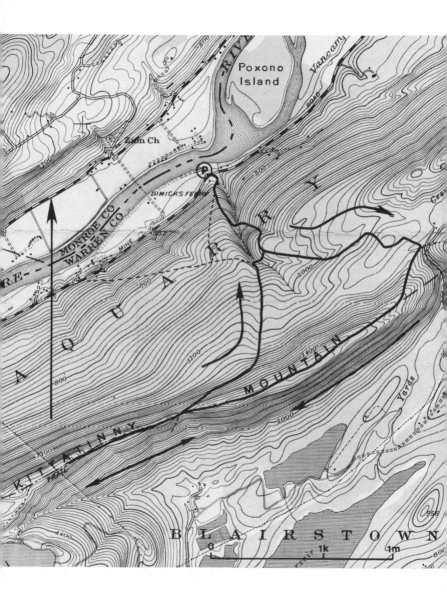

Poxono
Island

Zion Ch

MONROE CO
WARREN CO

DIMICKS FERRY

MINE

A Q U A R Y

K I T T A T I N N Y   M O U N T A I N

Yards

B L A I R S T O W N

0   1k   1m

start, after a brief descent, the Coppermines Trail meets the Appalachian Trail near Camp Road and Yards Creek.

At this junction, turn right (south) on the Appalachian Trail and climb steadily, steeply in places, to what is sometimes known as Raccoon Ridge. A little over half a mile from the junction, there is a good viewpoint to the left of the trail, and there is a second viewpoint to the left 500 feet further along the trail. Then, after another mile, you'll come to a series of open grassy areas, with views to the left over Yards Creek Reservoir, directly below.

About half a mile beyond these open spots, the trail descends briefly. Just before the trail begins to climb again, look for Kaiser Road, a blue-blazed woods road that comes in diagonally on the right. Although this road will be your return route, you should continue ahead on the Appalachian Trail for another 0.7 mile, over a series of rises, to the final, wide-open summit of Mt. Mohican, where there are good views of the Delaware Valley and Pennsylvania to the west.

After enjoying the vista, retrace your steps back to Kaiser Road, now on your left, and follow this blue-blazed trail downhill. After about a mile of easy walking, you'll come to a trail junction. Leave the road here and turn right, following the blue blazes. You'll cross two brooks and rejoin the red-blazed Coppermines Trail in about 0.2 mile. Make a left here and begin your descent into the gorge you passed through earlier. The red markers will lead back the way you came to the trailhead and your car.

25 Delaware Water Gap

> **General Description:** A strenuous uphill hike to a dramatic overlook on Mt. Tammany, a long walk on lightly used trails in a remote area, and a descent from a glacial lake.
>
> **Type of Trail:** Woods roads and rocky footpaths, with a particularly rocky ascent.
>
> **Distance:** 10.4 miles
>
> **Hiking Time:** 6-7 hours
>
> **Lowest Elevation:** 350 feet
>
> **Highest Elevation:** 1,540 feet
>
> **USGS Quad:** Portland, Bushkill
>
> **Other Maps:** NYNJTC Kittatinny Trails — Map #15, NJ Walk Book Map #15

Many New Jerseyans get their first taste of mountain hiking in the Delaware Water Gap area. It's easy to reach by car, and there are steep climbs, overlooks and a scenic glacial pond. What more could you ask for? As you might already suspect, this is a heavily used area, and parking may be limited on peak weekends.

Some may remember what this area, particularly the Appalachian Trail along Dunnfield Creek, looked like during the late 1960s. Tents everywhere, the smell of *canabis sativa* in the air, the sounds of the Grateful Dead, and of course, hundreds, perhaps thousands, of empty beer containers. Well, times have changed and, fortunately, scenes like this are a thing of the past. Today, there is a designated camping site (for thru-hikers on the A.T. only), monitored by the park rangers, and a more complete trail system that disperses hikers. In spite of (or, perhaps, because of) these newer, more restrictive regulations, the great beauty and vastness of the area remains and invites exploration. Both the State of New Jersey (Worthington State Forest) and the National Park Service (Delaware Water Gap National Recreation Area) manage the region. Except for the summit of Mt. Tammany and the area just to the north, this entire hike traverses Worthington State Forest.

The circuit hike described below is strenuous and is recommended only for those with experience, good endurance and sound woods sense. Those who wish to see some of the sights of this area but do not have the time or energy to take such a long hike should stop at the visitor center, get some maps and ask the park rangers for suggestions.

Trailhead: Take Interstate Route 80 west towards the Delaware Water Gap. About a mile before the bridge over the Delaware River, take an exit that leads to a rest area. Continue past the rest area parking, go past an underpass beneath Route 80 on the left, and turn right into a second parking area marked with a sign "Dunnfield Creek Natural Area." (If you miss the exit from Route 80, take the last exit in New Jersey, follow signs to the visitor center, and turn left, back under Route 80, to reach the parking area.)

Directions: Near the entrance to the parking area, on the right, a sign marks the start of the red-dot-on-white-blazed Mt. Tammany Trail. Follow this trail up some steps, and soon join another branch of the trail which comes up from the rest area parking. In another 500 feet, a set of rock steps marks the beginning of a steeper ascent. After turning off a woods road, the trail reaches a magnificent overlook over the Water Gap at 0.4 mile. Although there will be broader views from higher up, this viewpoint provides the best views up and down the river.

The grade now moderates somewhat, but in another 0.3 mile it steepens again, ascending first on switchbacks and then more steeply over a talus slope. This is the steepest part of the hike, and you will want to take your time climbing over these rocks. Finally, one mile from the start of the hike, you'll reach another viewpoint to the right. This a good place to take a breather. Although you still have some elevation to gain before reaching the summit, the toughest part of the hike is now over.

The trail now turns left and continues to climb, but on a more moderate grade. In another 0.3 mile, a path leading downhill to the right leads to the final overlook over the Water Gap, near the summit of the mountain. You can see the Indian Head rock formation across the river on Mt. Minsi, and you may also see hawks circling overhead and recreational boaters on the river below. Here, the Mt. Tammany Trail ends, and the Blue Trail begins. After you've spent some time checking out the view, continue ahead on the Blue Trail — now level, for a change!

You've now begun a 3.4-mile stretch of level, ridgetop walking along the crest of Mt. Tammany. There are views to the right over the Delaware River, with the concrete-arch bridge across the river an especially prominent feature. This railroad bridge was constructed by the Lackawanna Railroad about 1910. Although it has been abandoned for about 25 years, plans are underway to reinstate passenger service to Scranton, Pa. on this line.

Depue Island

PENNSYLVANIA
NEW JERSEY

Woodcock Bar

Labar I

SunFish Pd.
1382

H A Q U A R R Y

STATE FOREST AND PARK AREA

UNDEVELOPED

Creek

APPALACHI

M O U N T A I

After 0.3 mile, you will come a junction where the Blue Trail turns left. Do not turn left here; rather, continue ahead on a path which follows along the ridge. Maps label this route as the "Mt. Tammany Fire Road," but this section is no longer used as a fire road and has narrowed to a footpath. The first part may be indistinct in places, but for the most part, the route is fairly well defined and can be followed with care. You will notice some old, blacked-out blazes on trees along the route. The area you are passing through was burned by a forest fire in recent years. There are few mature trees, and the ground is covered, for the most part, with ferns, blueberry bushes and grass.

After about a mile and a half of this pleasant walking along the ridge, you will come to an open area, where a sign to the left marks the site of a heliport for the New Jersey Forest Fire Service. This spot is just north of the boundary between the Delaware Water Gap National Recreation Area (to the south) and Worthington State Forest (to the north). From here north, the fire road is dual-tracked, and it shows some signs of minimal use. In another quarter of a mile, a sign on a tree to the left indicates that you have traveled 2.2 miles from the Delaware Water Gap (the reference is to the distance from the last rocky overlook near the summit, where the Blue Trail begins).

Continue ahead for another 1.2 miles to a trail junction marked with a faint blue arrow, pointing left, painted on a rock. Turn left here and follow a clearly defined footpath through an open area. You are now on the Turquoise Trail, marked by light blue blazes, which you will be following for the next 1.3 miles. The trail soon begins a steady descent. After crossing a stream in a rocky area, it proceeds uphill to the Sunfish Pond Fire Road. Unlike the fire road along the ridge, this is a wide, maintained woods road. The Turquoise Trail turns left here and follows the fire road south for 0.3 mile, then turns right, leaving the road, and descends through mountain laurel. Sunfish Pond soon comes into view on the left.

As you approach the northeast corner of this beautiful glacial pond, the trail crosses an open area overlooking the pond. You've now covered nearly six miles, and this spot is an attractive place to take a much needed rest. After you've paused for a while, continue ahead, and you'll soon come to the terminus of the Turquoise Trail at a junction with the white-blazed Appalachian Trail (A.T.). Turn left onto the A.T., which you will follow for 4.4 miles back to the parking area.

The A.T. continues along the shore of the pond, following a rocky footpath for much of the way. You will notice a number of interesting rock sculptures to the left — the work of some enterprising hikers. In two-thirds of a mile, the A.T. reaches the southwest end of the pond, where a monument to the right commemorates the designation of Sunfish Pond in 1970 as a Registered Natural Landmark.

From here, the route back to your car is almost all level or downhill, although it is quite rocky in places. When you reach the Backpacker Site, be sure to bear left, following the white blazes of the A.T. (the woods road which continues ahead is the blue-blazed Douglas Trail). About a mile further on, an open area on the left allows a view over the Kittatinny Ridge, which you followed earlier in the hike.

After four miles on the A.T., you'll reach a junction with the Blue Trail up Mt. Tammany and the green-blazed Dunnfield Trail in the gorge of Dunnfield Creek. You have less than half a mile to get back to the parking area, but this gorge — with its cascades and towering trees — is one of the most beautiful parts of the hike. After crossing a wooden bridge, the trail passes a water pump and reaches the parking area where you began the hike.

Delaware Water Gap

Preface

For this fifth edition of *Circuit Hikes in Northern New Jersey*, all of the hikes were thoroughly rechecked by Trail Conference members Fred Hafele and Daniel Chazin. Daniel Chazin also served as the editor of the book. I would also like to thank Adrienne Coppola, who redesigned the book and produced the final copy on her computer, and Steve Butfilowski, who created the beautiful cover.

For this edition, significant changes have been made to many of the hike descriptions, although the hike routes themselves have not been altered, with one exception. Hike #9, The Wyanokie Plateau, is a completely different hike from the one which appeared in the fourth edition. I was compelled to make this change because the private landowner has closed some of the trails that were used by the previous hike. Fortunately, the new Hike #9 also passes many beautiful and interesting locations in the Wyanokies. Another change is that Hike #25, Delaware Water Gap, now proceeds in the opposite direction. The hiker now climbs the steep Mt. Tammany Trail at the start of the hike, rather than having to descend a very steep route at the end.

I am pleased that *Circuit Hikes* is being published in partnership with the New York-New Jersey Trail Conference, a volunteer organization which maintains many of the trails described in the book. It is through the efforts of the Trail Conference that such endangered areas as Pyramid Mountain have been protected and are now open to all for hiking. I encourage all hikers to support this organization and purchase their informative publications.

Bruce Scofield

CIRCUIT HIKES - KEY MAP

1. Watchung Reservation
2. The Great Swamp — Lord Stirling Park
3. South Mountain Reservation
4. High Mountain
5. Jockey Hollow
6. Pyramid Mountain/Tripod Rock
7. Ramapo Mountain State Forest
8. Ringwood State Park
9. The Wyanokie Plateau
10. The Torne
11. Bearfort Mountain
12. Terrace Pond
13. Pequannock Watershed — Bearfort Fire Tower
14. Pequannock Watershed — Buckabear Pond
15. Wawayanda State Park
16. Mahlon Dickerson Reservation
17. Allamuchy Mountain State Park
18. Hacklebarney State Park
19. Jenny Jump State Forest
20. High Point State Park
21. Stony Brook/Firetower Circular
22. Buttermilk Falls/Blue Mountain
23. Blue Mountain Lake
24. Coppermines and Mt. Mohican
25. Delaware Water Gap